KIMBERLY J. STAMATELOS

LifeInBalance Publishing
West Des Moines, Iowa
Copyright © 2014

LifeInBalance Publishing
West Des Moines, IA 50266
www.thecompassionatelawyers.com

Printed in the United States of America

Cover Design by William Love

Book Design by WORDART, West Des Moines, Iowa

DEDICATION

To my father, Dan Stamatelos, with love.
May his memory be eternal.

TABLE OF CONTENTS

Discourage litigation. Persuade your neighbors
to compromise whenever you can. As a peacemaker
the lawyer has superior opportunity of being a good
man. There will still be business enough.

- Abraham Lincoln

PART I

Chapter 1

Introduction:
My Journey To The Law

I am the child of a lawyer.

I remember my Dad wearing black horn rimmed glasses, a stylish suit with a pressed shirt, and a classy tie. He had a distinct spot of gray, the size of a quarter, right in the middle of his jet-black hair. He was a handsome Greek man – olive-skinned, medium height, and a prominent nose. When I picture him in my mind, I always, always, see him smiling.

His father, my grandfather John, owned a restaurant, Johnny's Vet's Club, in our small Iowa town. It was a haven for important movers and shakers of the time. As a young girl, my family and I spent a lot of time there. During the Iowa caucuses, the politicians and their entourages would come to "the club" to eat. I remember my Dad socializing and interacting with them and others in the community who frequented the restaurant. I always felt as a child that people liked my Dad, who they all referred to as "Danny," and that many thought he was important. Now, as an adult reflecting back, I recognize that in addition to his warm personality and way with people, part of what made Dad prominent was his title as "the lawyer."

As a teen, I earned extra money working at Dad's office, answering the phone and greeting the interesting people who came to see him. His clients were of all socioeconomic backgrounds, colors, and genders. Some dressed in suits while others wore work uniforms and had grease on their hands. Our part of town, known affectionately as Valley Junction, was a melting pot and Dad was at home among the various ethnic groups. I remember a Hispanic friend once remarked to me, "Danny was politically correct before it was cool to be politically correct."

Dad never turned away clients, even if they could only pay $10 a month on their bill. He often reached into his own pocket to help clients, sometimes paying their utility bill or doing something else to help them survive.

When I think about my Dad, I cannot recall everything with clarity, but the same thing always sticks with me. I remember, perfectly, the way my Dad would treat all people who crossed his path – a stranger, a client, a church member, even another lawyer. He treated everyone genuinely, with dignity and respect, and would listen as though he had all the time in the world. When I worked in the office, people didn't always come for legal problems. People came to see Danny for any problem. If anyone had a family issue, a problem with his mortgage, or a disturbed peace of mind, Danny was the first person they'd consult. My Dad had a connection in every walk of life, including doctors, bankers, and insurance men. He could make a simple phone call to help someone refinance, connect someone with a doctor, or brainstorm a next step. Regardless of the specifics, Dad would dispense the most important medicine: hope.

The atmosphere of Dad's small law firm was warm and welcoming. Not only did clients come in and out of the office, but Dad also allowed law students to come hang around the office. Even when the practice did not demand the staffing, he would put them to work in some way.

Ultimately, I became a lawyer myself. As I look back, I realize that watching my Dad over the years shaped me into the person and lawyer I am today. Having watched him I knew I wanted to "help people." I thought every lawyer was what I saw in my father. He was a compassionate lawyer.

My journey

I was always studious, graduating from high school a semester early at age 17. Dad convinced me to attend undergraduate at his alma mater,

Drake University in Des Moines, Iowa. I have always had wanderlust, so after my first year, I transferred to Arizona State University. At the time, I had no idea of my direction in life. I was taking courses simply to find my path. Eventually I enrolled in a course in criminal justice. A woman lawyer, who used a hornbook as our text, taught the class. I was immediately intrigued, both by the teacher and the subject matter. She was a bright professor and fit my impression of the ideal lawyer. I had a fleeting thought about pursuing the legal profession.

Ultimately, due to excessive partying and a falling grade point at ASU, I transferred back to Drake, finishing my entire undergrad in three years. My college credits all coalesced into a sociology degree, but I had no burning strategy for my life. Although my parents were proud that I was an accomplished student, neither of them, at any point in my education, discussed my future nor provided specific guidance. I had no real vision for myself.

When I told my Dad I was floundering, he suggested I go to law school. He delivered a pretty convincing pitch; it was a good way to make a living, he enjoyed the work, and "you never know what's going to walk in the door next." My Dad's encouragement convinced me to consider the idea of attending law school.

I felt responsible for taking the initiative to move forward and navigate the application process myself. I picked up a brochure at Drake on how to prep for the Law School Admissions Test (LSAT) and made a half-hearted attempt to review it. I hardly studied for the test, but still got a good score. My LSAT score was the first of many small seren-dipitous events that convinced me the law was the path for me.

Around the time I was putting together my application for Drake Law School, I was with my parents at a Drake football game. I struck up a conversation with the white-haired woman sitting next to me. When she questioned my career goals, I expressed to her my lackluster interest in becoming a lawyer. As I spoke she nodded and listened, being genuinely interested in hearing me speak my heart and under-standing what I was going through. I remember feeling comfortable conversing with this woman and most importantly that she had cared about my story.

As the game wrapped up, I vividly remember her looking me in the eyes saying, "I am Jan Reynoldson. I am a lawyer and my husband Ward is the Chief Justice of the Iowa Supreme Court. I'd like to write you a letter of recommendation to Drake Law School. You will be a marvelous lawyer. Will you allow me to write the recommendation?" My heart began pulsing as I tried to recall everything I had just said. I happily accepted, hardly knowing what her offer even meant. All I knew was that my life's events had put me on the road to applying to law school and two people, my Dad and this woman lawyer, were the most interested in my path. They were both lawyers and warm, caring people.

A few months later I was accepted to Drake Law School. From the first day of classes, I felt as though I was in the wrong place. My expectation of law school was a place where you learned to be compassionate, listen to people and become a problem solver. Instead I spent three years learning how to argue, advocate (even when I didn't believe in my case), out-gun and out-think "opposing" counsel. I learned how to use old cases to resolve similar situations and how to convince a judge or jury that a client deserved similar or different treatment from the people described in the cases. It was a strange system to grasp, one that was the opposite of what I thought I'd signed up for.

My class, the class of 1981, contained a literal overflow of over-achieving Type A personalities, only a third of which were women. I thought I would fit right in, as I was always at the top of my class, a member of my high school national honor society, had excellent grades in my undergraduate work and was accomplished in other extracurricular activities. Instead, I began one of the most difficult times of my life where my insecurities, fears, and inadequacies rose to the top, like the foam on a perfect latte. I spent long days with my classmates, many of whom were aggressive, hard-driven, and focused on being the best and the brightest. I was a deer in the headlights.

The boring and tedious Socratic method made no sense to me. I constantly lived in terror that law professors would call on me resulting in humiliation in front of my peers. My professors were like those in the classic movie "The Paper Chase," including one who convinced us if we did not know Latin we would never make it to graduation. The professors required extensive preparation and expected everyone to be "on" at all times. I often thought about my criminal law class in my undergraduate studies when I actually understood and enjoyed the material, which was directly laid out to us by a brilliant professor.

In law school there was no enjoyment. The lawyers-to-be I was training with all seemed to be getting with the program of being swordfighters while I just wanted to sit and talk it out. Was this being a lawyer? Instead of training us to be like I'd seen my Dad help clients, I was in a world that was encouraging us to be the polar opposite. As a result, I piled on an inordinate amount of stress and fear. Depression and anxiety became my constant companions.

I persevered through the first year, receiving a low grade on my first written paper, which was shocking. I'd never received a low grade in my life, and I'd always been complimented for my creative writing. Legal writing was apparently the opposite of creative writing. Obviously I had another skill to un-learn. I did have a small victory when I was a 1L oral arguments finalist and secured a coveted place on the Drake Moot Court team. Yet, my depression continued to worsen.

During my second year I started seeing a psychiatrist who told me to stay home when I didn't feel like going to class. For a time, I stayed home and skipped a majority of my classes, falling further behind. I contemplated dropping out. When I found spurts of motivation I searched for outlines in the student underground and did my best to make sense of the material. Law students seek out and share the outlines from the "smart" students, much like today's young adults share music. The message seemed to be that someone smarter than you had busted the code of what was being taught and put it into an understandable format. If you got your hands on the right material you could hope their printed straightforward wisdom would get you through.

When I felt lost and discouraged I confided my miseries to Terry, another classmate. Terry and I had gone to high school together and he was always approachable. We shared the fact that his father was also a lawyer. We compared notes and learned we were both miserable and bemoaned our futures, wondering if it was all worth it.

My second year was bumpy, but I could see the light at the end of the tunnel. During my time at Drake more than 30 years ago, clinical classes weren't offered so I spent time at my Dad's office learning "real" lawyering. It seemed that without his guidance all I had was a lot of book knowledge and no practical experience. Dad's office was a safe place for me to ask questions. I worried that I would become a lawyer who didn't know how to practice law. Many law students had the same fear. It was analogous to unleashing a doctor without a residency. We had to learn the hard way; we learned on the job.

Toward the end of my second year, my friend Terry committed suicide. I heard the news that day when I got to school. I was numb and felt guilty, thinking maybe if I hadn't commiserated with him and had instead encouraged him, he might still be alive. I had his Wills and Trusts outline in my bag and it felt eerie. However, nobody seemed to mourn. There was no memorial service or counselors to talk with. Everyone continued to plow through, nose to the grindstone with nobody's misery being acknowledged or discussed. I was disoriented and I was hanging on by a thread. I called my Dad and told him I was dropping out of law school. He asked me to meet him later so we could "talk it out."

That evening we met at the Village Inn. I remember sitting in a booth by the front door, and over a plate of cold pancakes, drowning in maple syrup, I cried my heart out. My Dad sat across from me. He listened as I blubbered and expressed the disconnection I felt in law school. I did not want to be a lawyer and certainly wasn't cut out for the profession. I wasn't even finished with school and I was emotionally drained. Besides that, I felt inadequate, depressed, constantly anxious, and unintelligent. My Dad listened intently and with empathy. When I had no tears left, my Dad reached across the table and touched my hand.

"Just finish," he said, "Just finish the degree. You will never, ever have to practice law if you don't want to. But the law degree is an education and a gift that will serve you in whatever you choose to do with your life. Having a law degree gives you skills, credibility, power, and an education that nobody will ever take away from you. What you do with it will be your choice. But please, just dig deep and finish."

The next few days I weighed my options and considered my Dad's advice. I could quit law school and allow the last two years to be a waste, or I could continue and at least get the degree. I chose to continue, finding a reservoir of courage I never knew I had. I was pro-active, surrounding myself with a few good, supportive friends at school and keeping a positive mindset. Although at times I seemed to be living in the midst of a thick fog, I conquered and obtained my degree.

My next milestone was the bar exam which was only a month after graduation. I'd spent every spare ounce of energy to finish the course-work for the degree, and therefore I had no motivation when it came time to study for the bar. I did my best to study, devoting time when I felt like I had the ability to focus.

The day of the bar exam I was a nervous wreck. I hardly remember taking the test, and the whole day was a blur. I knew I was inadequately prepared, but again I conjured up the courage I had and sat through the hours-long exam. My exam was before the implementation of an automated multistate multiple choice exam, and was 100% essay. We wrote and wrote in longhand for hours for two days. The exams were graded the afternoon of the final day and the scores were posted at the law school that evening.

My Dad drove a law school girlfriend and me to school to check our scores. She and I sat in the car and sent my Dad into the school with the other students to check the numbers. My heart pounded as he approached the car. "One of you passed and one of you failed," he said. At first I thought he was joking. However, I knew he was serious when he turned and went back to double check. "Never mind," he said, "You both failed." I was stunned. It may have happened over thirty years ago, but I still see his face peeking in the rolled down window like it was yesterday.

I felt defeated; shame, disappointment, and numbness overtook my mind and body. I also had the unenviable task of informing my family and friends, the secretaries at Dad's law office, and my classmates that I had not passed the bar. Most of my classmates were moving on to be the lawyers they aspired to become. I, on the other hand, visited my Grandpa John, the restaurateur, who wrote me a check to sustain me for a month, and supported my decision to leave town until the dust settled. Like an unwed mother in the 1950's, I was sent out of town to carry my shame on my own. I had a friend whom I'd met at ASU that lived in Dallas, Texas. I made my way to Dallas and set up camp on her living room couch while I pondered what to do next.

Finding new life in Dallas

I was once told that you are a lawyer if you have a degree, but an attorney only if you have a license to practice. At this point I was somewhere in between. I couldn't get a law-related job, but I was over-qualified for most business jobs. Because I felt urgency for redemption, I applied for anything and everything I could find.

One day my Dad called. A Des Moines friend of his had a lawyer connection, Arthur, who lived in Dallas and needed an assistant to help sort through legal documents. I was thrilled at the thought of employment. As a favor, Arthur hired me as a law clerk to sort through documents, day after day on site at a franchise business his client was purchasing.

I knew I needed to stay in Dallas and could not go home until I had something to show for it. My family would have happily welcomed me, but I had a lot of shame to unload. I worked hard for Arthur. He had high expectations but gave me a fair shot. As I began a real world job, I realized that my years in law school had strengthened my work ethic. Arthur and I were thorough with our work and put in long hours. He was pleased with my efforts and validated me. I felt a true boost of confidence.

As our project came to a conclusion, I knew in the back of my mind that I needed to go back to Iowa and reattempt the bar exam. I flew home briefly, met my friend who had also failed, and we both successfully passed the Iowa bar. When I returned to Texas, Arthur offered to put in a call to Rodeway Inns International, a hotel chain where he had worked as general counsel. I was instantly excited, only to remember I had passed the Iowa Bar, not the Texas Bar. However, I was still interested and applied to run the franchise document administration for the company, a job that had previously been handled by a paralegal.

I accepted the position and worked hard to make a good impression, interacting with state regulators and developing new company procedures. As I became involved and networked within the company, I built up enough motivation to tackle and pass the Texas Bar exam. Soon thereafter, I approached my boss and suggested that I become corporate counsel for the company. We negotiated back and forth. I remember being so anxious about the idea of being corporate counsel that when he agreed, I settled for a pay that was less than ideal. A year later I pressed for the title of "General Counsel" and the company acquiesced. Although my pay was the same, I wanted that title. My ego needed the title to hold my own with my classmates who had launched into substantial careers.

As General Counsel I began feeling accomplished as a lawyer. I remember the company had free long distance calling. Nearly every morning I would go into my office, ask not to be disturbed, and close the door. I would immediately pick up the phone, call my Dad, and plead that he coach me through my task list. I was a "baby lawyer" who knew very little. I was the only lawyer in the company.

Although I enjoyed the corporate world, I felt that I wasn't a "real" lawyer unless I took my turn in the courtroom. However, women litigators were few and far between at the time. When a former law school classmate told me about an opening for a litigation attorney at his firm in Dallas, I applied and was offered a position. As the only woman in the litigation section, I was asked to serve the coffee to my male colleagues, and then brief the litigation team on cases. I could

9

have become defensive but I decided to serve up the hottest and most delicious coffee on Earth, and then sit at the table and learn everything I could from the experienced male trial attorneys. I look back and chuckle about how times have changed.

I became close friends with an associate at the firm, Jeffrey. He was married to another solo practice attorney, Lyla. At the time, I began dating my future husband, Bill, and the four of us became close friends. However, it didn't take me long to realize that I was not content at the firm, which continued my streak of unhappiness in the practice of law. While Jeffrey could skillfully maneuver the office politics, I was annoyed and discouraged. Other than Jeffrey, the attorneys were less than compassionate. I remember the way they would even demean clients, particularly a woman client who was involved in a suit for an injury. She was seriously burned and the lawyers would refer to her as "the crispy critter." I was disgusted and felt a pit in my stomach every time they made fun of the poor suffering woman. Once again, I felt uneasy in the practice of law and began to wonder whether I was suited to be a lawyer.

A few months later I heard about a restaurant chain, Chili's, which was hiring legal counsel. I opted back into corporate law again trying to find somewhere to fit in. I was immediately issued a coveted "green card" – I had unlimited access to free dining at any of the Chili's locations. When my family visited from Iowa I took them all to dinner. I could sense my parents' pride when I showed the waitress my green card. As a "big wig" for the company, we were always provided with exceptional service. During this time I hoped the stories of my accomplishments were being filtered back home to those who had labeled me as somehow "not enough" to be a good lawyer.

My boss, another in-house Counsel, was an easygoing lawyer. Too easy going. As time passed, she became less and less available for assistance and more difficult to work with. Later I found out she was operating a private practice on the side. My position became overly stressful. Chili's was into its growth years, and she was more often unavailable. When I approached her about the situation, she did not appreciate my complaint. She immediately scheduled a performance review and I was criticized for a variety of things. I refused to sign off on the performance evaluation because I didn't agree with her statements. Within the next few weeks I had more unscheduled performance evaluations, and I was ultimately fired for poor performance.

In my heart of hearts I knew I had a strong performance, or at least an acceptable one. She asked me to pack up and leave immediately when she told me I was terminated. I refused. Instead I walked into the CEO's office to inform him of my unfair treatment and that my supervising lawyer was spending time on other obligations. I also made him aware that my immediate departure would jeopardize my caseload. The CEO allowed me to stay to dictate a status report and promised to call me after he investigated the situation. Although the call never came, I did learn that the lawyer who had supervised me ultimately left the company.

Bill and I flew back to Iowa and got married in a big Greek wedding. A year later I was pregnant with our first daughter, Danielle. During this transitional time in my life, I maintained my close friendship with Lyla and Jeffrey. As lawyers we always discussed legal topics. One day Lyla announced she had found something in the back of the ABA Journal that piqued her interest; a man had opened a mediation firm in Seattle, Washington and was looking for lawyers to "buy in" to a network of lawyers that would become mediators. At the time, in 1986, I had never heard of mediation and I doubted the idea. Lyla was enthralled, and she and Jeffrey flew to Seattle to become trained in mediation. When they returned to Dallas, they became fully immersed.

Shortly after my termination at Chili's, I began my own solo practice in Dallas. Of all my legal experiences, my mind always resonated back to my Dad's office. I recollected the joy I saw on his client's faces leaving the office after coming in with a heavy burden. As I began my practice, I knew business would be slow, so I was willing to take whoever walked in the door as a client. Then one morning I came across an ad in the paper. A janitorial franchise firm was seeking general counsel. I called the CEO immediately and arranged a meeting, during which

I convinced him I could serve as his general counsel from my own office. He was thrilled with the idea, as he would not have to hire me as in-house counsel, but since I was just developing a solo practice I would have a lot of time to work on his legal issues. My previous franchise and corporate expertise was paying off.

I loved having my own practice, particularly the flexibility and knowing that I was ethically compliant. My janitorial firm client, Jim, was a family man of high integrity. His wife worked in the company and she was also warm and inclusive, inviting me to all the company functions and even to come to their family home and hang out around the swimming pool. I loved the work I did for them, personally and for the company. I felt like they were my extended family.

During this time I also met Judge Merrill Hartman, a state court judge in Dallas, Texas. He had set up a pro bono clinic at the Dallas Bethlehem Center. In the evenings, I would go there to represent indigent clients. Judge Hartman would also give me guidance on how to run my legal practice. I remember his important advice: always get a retainer. "A client who doesn't give you a retainer will not be able to pay you what you are worth as a lawyer," he said. In essence he showed me, through his actions, that a lawyer could make a good living and contribute time to pro bono as well. Judge Hartman is now deceased. In researching this book, I found that he continued being notable in Texas for his pro bono work. Interestingly, years after I had worked with him, he was also the first Texas judge to order mediation in family cases.

After giving birth to my daughter Danielle, I began to feel inordinate amounts of pressure; the demands of the practice, my husband being on the road all the time, and raising my colicky daughter. My husband agreed we would move back to Iowa to have the support of my family. My friend Lyla was understanding, and open to discussing my personal life and career decisions. She was adamant that I take the mediation franchise for Iowa. She knew I would love it. Solely on her recommendation, I made arrangements to become the Iowa officeholder of United States Arbitration and Mediation (USA&M).

When I returned home to Iowa, my Dad and his partner, Greg Kenyon, welcomed me to their practice of Stamatelos & Kenyon. I started to work in the areas of personal injury, probate, real estate and family law. In turn, I welcomed Iowa to a new concept: mediation.

Bringing mediation to Iowa

I was excited about mediation and hit the ground running. It seemed to be exactly what I was looking for when I went to law school. However, I only found three people out of all the lawyers I knew in Iowa, who were even remotely interested in the concept; a woman federal magistrate, Celeste; the manager of a grant being held by the Drake Legal Clinic, Beverly; and a local lawyer who was a litigator, Roger. The four of us met frequently to discuss the implementation and growth of mediation in Iowa.

Two men, Michael and Alan, ran the USA&M group. Alan came to Iowa and Minnesota to conduct mediation trainings. For our first training, I recruited a dozen or so lawyers who were half-heartedly interested. I recall my excitement for the first training and all the trainees that attended, but one trainee in particular: Dick. As the former Dean of Drake University Law School, Dick told me that day that he was attending as a favor to my Dad, his close personal friend. When Alan began conducting the training, it took me only a morning to see that what he was describing was revolutionary. I glanced around the room a few times to find Dick's head bowed down. I wondered if he was either sleeping or rummaging through the packet of materials. Then suddenly he came to life, raising his head with open eyes. He was riveted for the duration of the training and from that moment he fell in love with mediation. Dick had previously started the American Mock Trial Association and since Alan's training in mediation in the late 1980's has established several mediation organizations and tournaments, written several books on mediation, and has trained mediators in Ireland, Dubai, and India.

Ultimately, I acquired the US Arbitration & Mediation franchises for Iowa, Minnesota, North and South Dakota and Northern Illinois.

Thereafter, I presented the concept of mediation to the Iowa Supreme Court Continuing Legal Education (CLE) committee. Since mediation was a new concept I was opening new markets to the idea. As I built my panels of mediators in the five state region I traveled extensively, spending time presenting seminars to insurance companies and CLE attendees. At that time I was pregnant with our second daughter, Courtney, and I remember being hugely pregnant with swollen feet as I gave presentations all over the Midwest. My work in building mediation was exhilarating. I was using all of my lawyer skills: persuasion, public speaking, advocacy for my cause, and dissecting cases that my panels of mediators were settling. I felt competent, confident and inspired. I had found my niche and myself.

Initially, there was resistance to mediation. The legal community was skeptical of the idea. Defense lawyers feared that mediators were going to interfere with their ability to try cases and settle them on their own. Plaintiff's attorneys were unsure how their clients would fare in such an informal setting. I fought back the skeptics with the sense of courage I developed in law school and fueled by my passion for the process of mediation. In turn, the idea of mediation caught on like wild fire.

Roger and I worked together to establish a court connected mediation program in our judicial district under the control of the county bar association. Together we hired a man, Joe, a trained mediator, to administer the program. Beverly left the Drake Legal Clinic so I was hired to manage the grant she had been administering, setting up court connected mediation programs, and traveling the state of Iowa, conducting trainings and educating judges and lawyers. I had found the most exhilarating joy as a lawyer. Most importantly, I'd found mediation, and it seemed to be the way to resolve conflict I'd been looking for since law school.

Mediation was rolling in Iowa. I ran my mediation company for five years then sold my Iowa, Minnesota, and Dakotas franchises so my family could move to Chicago where my husband had been accepted into graduate school.

Quick stop in Chicago

My husband pursued a graduate degree at Northwestern while I continued to build the Chicago franchise office. I will always remember a cocktail party that my husband and I attended with the Northwestern law professors whom were part of the master's faculty. They sought me out, having read about my mediation companies in my husband's application and they were interested in hearing about it. I was ecstatic – law professors were seeking me out to learn about my business development accomplishments.

During this time I also gave birth to our son, Clint. For the duration of our time in Chicago, I trained some of the Cook County judges through the Drake grant. After two years, we decided to sell the last of the franchises and move to Scottsdale, Arizona, as I always had the burning desire to live there since my days at ASU.

Settling in Scottsdale

While in Scottsdale I continued to fulfill my obligations of the Drake grant. I flew back and forth to Iowa frequently to conduct training. During the years of implementing mediation, I did very little of the actual mediation work myself and preferred to be on the business and creative side of the developing market. My law degree and legal experience gave me credibility as I frequently spoke with lawyers, judges, and court administrators.

In the late 90's, JAMS/Endispute, the largest private mediation firm in the country based in Irvine, California, hired me to be Vice President of Business Development. I commuted to Irvine, California from Scottsdale a few days a week. Right when my career was at a pinnacle, I began facing crisis at home. My family, then three children and a husband, was crumbling. My husband had a busy career building an industrial engineering company, which required extensive travel. In the meantime, I was still commuting to Irvine a few days a week. The demanding travel took a toll on our relationship and our family.

One day I was sitting at my desk in California when I got a call from my son's elementary school in Scottsdale. No one had picked him up after school. Although we had a live in nanny holding down the fort, as a mother, I felt instant shame and failure. I immediately called my husband, only to find out that he had left for the east coast with the impression that I was returning home that day in time to pick up the kids. I was thankful for my close friend, Laura, who rescued my son. When I got back to Scottsdale that night I knew something had to give. The situation truly demonstrated the trade-off between a family and a demanding career, a problem faced by many lawyers trying to raise a family. I could not manage both. Although my husband and I were making the same money, it only seemed logical in those days that the woman be the one to quit and stay home. I quit JAMS/Endispute and gave up my career to put all my efforts toward my children and deteriorating marriage.

Shortly after my resignation, my father retired as a lawyer in Iowa. He and my mother moved to Arizona where they had a second home. I looked forward to having my parents around as I raised my children, but when my Dad got off the plane, he had a cold that seemed to never go away. My friend Laura's husband was an emergency room doctor and I arranged for him to see my Dad at the emergency room. I remember him hopelessly telling me, "Kim, your father is going to die." My mother could not face the fact that Dad was dying from an incurable lung disease, idiopathic pulmonary fibrosis. I had to stay strong and again find the courage to persevere, holding up all of us.

At the time I remained unemployed and was a stay at home mom, so I moved both of my parents into my home. For the next seven months, hospice nurses would come and go, and I began giving round-the-clock care to my Dad. My husband was on the road most of the time, my mother was overcome with grief, and my children needed assistance with homework and adolescent worries. Without intentions of doing so, I single-handedly set up a household to care for all the wounded.

During this time my Dad and I had many talks. I asked him if he enjoyed being a lawyer. He said he had LOVED his work as a lawyer. He told me that above all to remember the client judges the EFFORT a lawyer puts in on their behalf, more than the OUTCOME of a case.

The effort is what one can control. The outcome may often depend on the facts of the case, the judge or jury. I remember being envious that he seemed to have been so content and wondered if I would be able to say the same on my own deathbed.

Being face-to-face with death, I began to closely examine my own life. It was clear that my marriage had been lifeless for years. My attempts to quit my profession to save it were of no avail. I confided to my Dad that I planned to divorce my husband, Bill. Dad said, "I wish I could be here to help you," knowing his death was imminent. A year later, after my Dad passed away, I confronted Bill about the divorce and requested that we have a mediator handle the process.

I was pleased with the divorce mediation process, as the mediator was a lawyer, psychologist, and mediator all wrapped up in one. Where I went wrong, however, was in not having legal representation at the table. I was emotionally, physically, and spiritually depleted at the time, and most interestingly I wanted to avoid retaining and paying a lawyer. In turn, I was careless, walking away from assets and backing away from a viable alimony claim even though I was unemployed and my husband made a substantial income. I felt exhausted, alone, and in grief and I just wanted to get out of the marriage. As I reflect on the situation, I have developed a newfound respect for my clients that do not have much money but spend what they have to make sure I am representing them during the devastation of divorce. I also have a heightened sensitivity to my client's needs, particularly when it comes to billing.

After my divorce I struggled to find work in Scottsdale. I no longer had my Dad to console my worries and concerns or provide guidance. I hadn't taken the Arizona bar exam, there was no reciprocity for my Iowa license, and I had let my Texas license lapse. Law firms did not want me and I was overqualified for paralegal positions. The mediation market in Arizona was just beginning, but firms didn't know me because I did all my work outside of the state. It was hard to break into the legal community. I was at an all-time low. Believe it or not, I filled out an application and accepted a position as a barista at Starbucks. I was a lawyer working at Starbucks for health insurance, receiving no alimony, and having gone from an all-time high to one of the lowest parts of my life. How could I have done this to myself?

Take me home

I returned home to Iowa for a few weeks. Once again, courage was my saving grace. I tested the waters of the Iowa legal community to see if I could find employment. Within a week I reconnected with other lawyers and had an interview at a medium sized law firm.

While I had been gone from Iowa, the mediation movement I had helped plant there was going strong. The chief judge in our district, Judge Levine, had passed a local rule requiring mediation in family law cases and Joe (the man I'd helped hire) had done a wonderful job at managing the program. When I met the partners at my interview, there were many I had previously trained in mediation. Some were still actively mediating and made a point to acknowledge the difference I had made in helping to bring mediation to Iowa. I felt validated being in Iowa again and accepted the job with the firm.

My career was about to pick up again. The firm encouraged me to build my mediation practice. I also had a desire to start my own family law practice, largely because of my own divorce experience and a new affinity for divorcing people that needed legal representation. After two years at the firm, I left to build my solo family law and mediation practice.

Dick, one of my first mediation trainees, by then had developed a nationwide mediation practice, and he convinced me to share office space with him. I began teaching mediation at Drake Law School as an adjunct professor, and hired one of my former students as an associate. I felt like everything was coming together. I was in the right place, doing what the law called me to do, and being the lawyer I was meant to be. My professional life was outstanding, but my personal life took another devastating blow.

While I was reconstructing my professional life, I dated and ultimately married another man. Unfortunately, it didn't take me long to realize I'd made a horrible mistake. In retrospect I realize that at the time of my second marriage, I was grieving the death of my father, feeling guilt from the demise of my first marriage, and I was trying to reclaim my professional life authentically. I was in no shape to be entering a new marriage. After a failed attempt at marriage counseling, one day I tearfully typed up my divorce papers. It was déjà vu. A close lawyer friend represented me. I was divorced 90 days later. Although the process was easier the second time, the emotional wound was tremendously deeper.[1]

I continued my family law practice and the way I dealt with clients changed drastically. When my clients had to leave marital homes, share co-parenting of children with exes who were still angry, and face fears of the future, it touched me deeply. I could easily relate to their feelings. I took major, courageous pro-active steps in healing myself, physically, mentally, and spiritually. I accepted myself and stood firmly in my authentic life as a lawyer. I chose to practice from a place of compassion, and expanded my practice to include collaborative law, mediation, parenting coordination and some litigation.

I gathered like-minded collaboratively trained professionals and we formed a collaborative law practice group, meeting monthly in my office. We brought in nationally acclaimed trainers and held a training workshop for lawyers, counselors and financial professionals to expand the collaborative practice. I also helped establish a practice group of parenting coordinators to meet monthly and explore how to improve on the parenting coordination process, and develop standard protocols to enhance the effectiveness of the practice.[2]

Continuing to teach mediation at the law school, I restructured the course so that the students would mediate cases for indigent clients at the Volunteer Lawyers Program after they had been trained in mediation during class. On the last day of class the students deal with these clients directly, providing access to legal services and also enhancing their compassionate lawyering skills.

Additionally, I took life coaching training and started to coach law students and lawyers, meeting monthly and then having them send weekly accountability emails. Investing time in these lawyers and lawyers-to-be has been one of my greatest joys. I also have law students come to observe my practice and shadow me in mediation.

I currently own a thriving law and mediation practice and take part in the growing integrative law movement.[3] Over time I've realized that as a lawyer, I am uniquely situated to touch a client's life at their most vulnerable moments. As that lawyer, I do my best to lead clients to the most important outcomes: courage and hope. By stabilizing my mind, body, and spirit, for the first time in my life, I had the ability to be my authentic self. Like my Dad, I strive to be a compassionate lawyer.

My hope is that through my journey to become a compassionate lawyer and the discoveries I have made about the legal practice along the way, I will have an impact on the legal profession. Most importantly, my hope is that I can remind lawyers from all walks of the profession of the higher calling for us as lawyers. We are called to be conduits of healing for our client. What we do with them, when we find them in the midst of their story, MATTERS DEEPLY. And for those lawyers who feel like they have lost their way, caught up in a noble profession that has somehow also lost its way, it is not too late.

Our profession is calling lawyers home. Perhaps by talking about and describing the compassionate lawyer, we will release more of them on a hurting world. Lawyers who are reading this book, will you join us?

Chapter 2

Who Are The Lawyers?

I truly love lawyers.

I have been around them my entire life, and as a result, I have watched them. My observations lead me to believe that there aren't many lawyers who drive their practices from a place of compassion.

To place a call to compassion on the profession, I first had to identify where to call lawyers *from*. So I developed a rubric to categorize lawyers.

First, I decided to break them into categories based on their motivation. Were they more interested in profit or service? Were they more interested in themselves or others? I placed the lawyer on the rubric and provided a name for each type of lawyer, but not in a derogatory manner, because it is not my intention to disparage lawyers. Instead, the rubric is meant to show lawyers a simplistic base of their legal practices. From there they can decide if they want to move toward compassion.

With this guideline, I developed the following chart:

Self

Profit (Winning)	Pragmatic	Benevolent
	Generous	Compassionate

Profit
(Winning) — on left

Service
(Justice) — on right

Others
(Client)

Next, I developed seven standards by which to measure each lawyer. Those standards are:

1. How well does the lawyer operate from wholeness of mind, body, and spirit?

2. Does the lawyer have genuine care and empathy for the people they serve?

3. Is the lawyer respectful of self, family, colleagues, the court, and others?

4. Does the lawyer live and lead well, empowering experienced lawyers and mentoring the younger generation of lawyers?

5. Does the lawyer use their unique legal skills and wisdom in their philanthropic work?

6. Does the lawyer have a fair and just billing practice and a healthy relationship with money?

7. Is the lawyer working to create change and innovation in the legal profession for the common good?

After putting the various lawyer styles into the four categories, I rated them in more detail according to the seven standards. I interviewed many lawyers and judges about how they perceived themselves and their colleagues. The following descriptions are overviews of the four types of lawyers I categorized. Each profile is not of one particular lawyer, but is a combination of the qualities.

Lawyers are often chameleons, changing their approach and persona to suit the job that needs to be done. They can argue one side of a case today, then take a totally different position on another case tomorrow, depending on the needs of the clients. So, to place all lawyers into one category is impossible.

Each of us has a *deferential* manner of doing business – the style we use under pressure or in the face of an adversary. However, more than likely we each have a *preferred* style that is more authentic. The tension that comes with many lawyers is that we operate so often in our deferential manner that we lose touch with our preferred style, creating an internal paradox that is an undoing for many of us.

My personal belief is that we have all been uniquely wired to feel most authentic as a compassionate lawyer; however, we have moved away from compassion after years of escalating to aggression, the norm of the legal profession. If you are a lawyer, as you read this book perhaps you can use the tools to move back to your authentic self; a lawyer who drives your practice of law from a place of compassion. You can reclaim the Compassionate Lawyer. If you are a consumer of legal services, perhaps this will be a guide to help you identify a compassionate lawyer to assist you with your legal issues.

Profile #1: The pragmatic lawyer

Henry is the senior partner of a law firm that bears his name. He has the large corner office in the elaborate suite, adorned with fine furniture and art. Henry is well known, not only by lawyers, but by everyone in town. If you asked someone in the community to describe him, it is likely you would hear words like aggressive, a pitbull, ruthless, and intimidating. Henry is proud of this definition, citing that a lawyer's goal is to win; and he does win.

Unwilling to compromise the quality of his work, Henry spends long hours at the firm and often eats processed or easily available foods on a sporadic basis, washing it down with bottles of diet soda. He doesn't sleep soundly or fully, but delights in the fact he doesn't require much sleep. Recently, Henry started to work out at the YMCA lifting weights after he stopped exercising long ago. He believes strength is important. He does not belong to or attend a house of worship and would most likely define himself as agnostic, although other members of his family claim a religious affiliation. It is apparent that self-care is not on Henry's radar.

Henry handles his clients with an iron hand. It is "his" case and he strongly believes clients are paying for his judgment. If clients want a listening ear or care and empathy, they should go to a counselor. In mediation, Henry rarely allows his client to speak, even if in a confidential private caucus with the mediator. If clients aren't listening to him, Henry is not afraid to yell at them, berate them, or tell them they are being stupid. If they continually fail to take his advice, he may withdraw from their case. If it is too late to withdraw, Henry will zealously advocate for his clients with his finest skills. However, behind the scenes Henry makes his clients miserable, leaving them to regret they have held him hostage in this manner. Henry always plays to win – it was that way even when playing monopoly as a kid. Surrender is a sign of weakness.

The fear of a legal grievance doesn't intimidate Henry. He is the first to call himself "a damn good lawyer" and he is secure that he can defend any attacks on his ethics or the quality of his work. He wouldn't dream of settling or mediating a complaint about his work or his billing practices. He personally shows up at any administrative proceedings on such matters to confront the accuser face-to-face and to raise issues about the client's behavior or attitude before the tribunal. Henry is likely to engage in retaliatory collection practices after successfully defending a grievance.

With his colleagues, Henry does what is necessary to provide him with a competitive advantage, sacrificing respect if it is necessary. If an opposing lawyer asks for a continuance, he rarely agrees. If it is due to something like death or illness he may agree, but it is not always guaranteed. Henry quickly files motions, such as a motion to compel discovery, if opposing counsel misses a deadline in conformance with a rule – and Henry doesn't back down unless sanctions or fees are discussed and reconciled. He is always over-prepared for a case because of the extra help from his assistants. Henry has a zero tolerance policy for other lawyers who are not as exceptionally prepared as he is. Those other lawyers receive the brunt of his aggressive practices.

Bar committees, social committees and cultural boards are not

Henry's style. His work is his life and it leaves very little time for him to engage in much else. Plus, he is not a social person, although he has extreme loyalty to the lawyers in his firm. Henry's family complains that he has very little time for them, and it's true.

Henry's policy for the young lawyers at the firm is an open door policy, but anyone that asks for his time must come with specific questions and an agenda to make maximum use of his time. He is too busy to simply sit and discuss anything else with any lawyers, inside or outside his firm. If a law student or young lawyer approached him about a formal mentoring relationship, his secretary would likely say he is too busy.

Henry sets no pro bono or public service policy for himself or his firm. If a lawyer in his firm wants to do pro bono work, Henry allows it as long as the lawyer's required billable time is met and as long as pro bono work isn't "excessive." However, he by no means encourages pro bono or any type of philanthropic endeavors. Henry would prefer his lawyers were out in public, in roles of high visibility, and in social circles where they may interface with potential wealthy clients. As for himself, Henry finds pro bono clients difficult to manage and without the threat of fees to manage them, it would be too frustrating of an endeavor to make it meaningful. He makes charitable contributions to his friends who serve on boards when they "hit him up" for a check. He carries more than his share of overhead at the firm and provides generously for his children, and even nieces and nephews, to be educated at the finest universities.

Henry's fees are some of the highest in town and much higher than many lawyers who are similarly situated. He will not take a case without a substantial retainer, which is also higher than most of his counterparts, and he doesn't hesitate to demand more retainer if the initial one runs low. If the money becomes a problem, Henry fires the client and has no problem in filing a suit to collect the fees owed to him. If he knows the client has the funds or a particular client has annoyed him, Henry's collection practices can be particularly aggressive. He can recite a list of clients he has forced into bankruptcy in retaliation for their attitude toward paying him and in their attitude toward him in particular. He doesn't hesitate to encourage clients to sell things to pay him, or to get a lien on their house.

After any case, Henry uses what he calls his "bathtub brain" – his brain was full at the time of advocacy and he drains it when the case is over. He never thinks about a client afterwards and if a client needs him later, a retainer is involved and it can only be for a specific legal matter. Henry learned his ways as a young lawyer. Nobody mentored him, so he had to learn from the school of hard knocks. He spent hours at the courthouse watching trials, looking through case files, and reading the law. He never reached out to another older or more experienced lawyer and he does not discuss his cases with other colleagues even to this day. Henry believes a real lawyer has the "guts" to jump in and work hard to figure things out on his own. A lawyer is not a role model, but a professional that commands respect and fear. Henry admits the ego is very motivating.

Henry has no interest in innovating or using his years of experience and wisdom to contribute to the profession. As far as he is concerned, everyone entering the law should have to go through what he went through. Even if the Socratic method is boring and useless, young lawyers should have to pay their dues. Henry has no interest in integrative law practices such as mediation, collaborative law, or other peacemaking methods. The courtroom is the only place where justice can be found in Henry's mind. He has no interest in changing the status quo in the law.

In summary, here is how the Pragmatic Lawyer sits within the seven criteria for compassionate lawyering:

1. **Compassion for self**
   The lawyer works long hours, often skipping meals or eating processed foods at the office. It is routine for the lawyer to have a few cocktails every night and to struggle with sleep issues. He or she may exercise sporadically, but is disconnected from the body except as a source of

power. This lawyer does not live in the present moment
and has no spiritual or relaxation practice, and is not
awake or aware of being on a journey of self.

2. **Care and empathy**
   The lawyer believes clients are paying for legal judgment
   and aggressive representation only; therefore, the case is
   the lawyer's case, not the client's. He or she identifies the
   lawyer's role as obtaining the best outcome for a client and
   has the attitude that if clients need a listener or empathetic
   heart, they should go to a counselor.

3. **Respectful**
   The lawyer does not socialize with other lawyers except
   lawyers who he or she practices with–those who have a
   direct financial impact on his or her practice (example,
   junior associates). This lawyer is always extraordinarily
   prepared for any case, court hearing, or trial. He or she
   treats the court with respect, but often files motions when
   a result is rendered for the opposing party. The lawyer has
   little or no time for collegiality with an adversary and will
   use aggressive practices if it means competitive advantage.

4. **Empowers other lawyers**
   The lawyer has no time to serve as a mentor and does not
   have a mentor of his or her own. He or she is available to
   associates at the firm, as long as time permits. The lawyer
   does not have any formal relationship with an accountability partner or other lawyers.

5. **Philanthropy with lawyer skills**
   The lawyer has no time for public service because he
   or she is too busy. Instead, he or she may write a check
   to charitable causes if solicited from someone he or she
   knows. The lawyer is not interested in pro bono work
   because the clients are too high maintenance.

6. **Fair and just**

   The lawyer bills some of the highest rates in town and bills for incidentals such as copies, faxes, and other administrative tasks. He or she uses aggressive collection practices, especially against certain ungrateful or arrogant clients.

7. **Legacy for the future**

   The lawyer has no interest whatsoever in the future of the profession. He or she believes things in the law are good as they are and should not change. The lawyer does not take an interest in legal trends or discussion of legal topics other than reading current case law.

Pros and cons of pragmatic-style lawyering

Pros:

1. The Pragmatic has all the trappings of legal opulence. The lawyer's office is elegant, the support staff is well trained, and the Pragmatic makes so much money he or she doesn't ever go without, and his or her ego is fed regularly.

2. Pragmatics don't have to worry whether justice prevails because they are only concerned with the "win." If they are victorious in a case, they consider it a job well done, regardless of the consequences of the battle. The Pragmatics' clients are required to get in line with their strategy.

3. Because winning is the be-all and end-all, taking aggressive steps to lead to the end doesn't phase the Pragmatic. As long as it is within the canons of ethics, the Pragmatic is comfortable with what he or she has to do to get the best outcome.

4. Pragmatics are often feared by other attorneys because they use intimidation as part of their repertoire. The Pragmatic is always prepared, knows their way around a courthouse, and is in command of their work and personal lives.

5. If they want to undertake philanthropic causes they are able to write big checks or take advantage of other alternatives, such as buying tables at important community functions.

6. Pragmatics make lots of money. They may say money is not a primary driver, but they acknowledge that having lots of money is an ego boost. Pragmatics know they are worth the high fees they charge.

7. The Pragmatic knows that after they retire or die, their name will still be notorious for lawyers to come in the future. Their name will most likely carry on in the firm name for years to come.

Cons:

1. Pragmatics acknowledge "the law is a jealous mistress" and may regret they have no time to do activities and family events. They may have even forgotten how to have fun. Pragmatics are often plagued by health and sleep problems due to poor self-care. They may run from an emptiness that they can't identify deciding that if they just keep working and winning, they won't have to face it.

2. Clients that hire Pragmatics often dislike or disparage the lawyer after the matter is completed. Some clients feel abused by the lawyer.

3. Pragmatic lawyers are often wedded to the traditional practice of law. They rarely do creative problem solving for clients. They think in terms of black and white and not "outside the box." Pragmatics are driven by cases and statutes.

4. The Pragmatic lawyers are often loners as they rarely have a sense of collegiality and often have limited or no

social circle beyond their family and a few close friends. Pragmatics don't share their wisdom. They are often the most brilliant lawyers but they aren't likely to write books or teach or mentor younger lawyers. As a result, other lawyers do not benefit from the pragmatic's knowledge.

5. Because they are financially secure and often have vast support staffs to handle their work, the Pragmatics are often the best suited to help in pro bono efforts. However, they rarely roll up their sleeves to work with underprivileged or groups who may not have access to justice.

6. When clients disrespect Pragmatics, don't pay them, or don't value the outcome reached for them, Pragmatics may over-react, often causing stress and negative repercussions. These lawyers often have fragile egos hidden behind their drive for winning and making money.

7. These lawyers don't pass on their gifts to the future of the profession, often feeling that they had to do it the hard way and others should have to as well. Having seen the traditional practice of law from a front row seat, they are often the most equipped to recognize where changes could benefit the system but they are not interested in leaving a legacy.

Profile #2: The generous lawyer

Sean is a well-known, and well-liked member of the legal community. He always looks like a million dollars, dressing in beautiful custom made suits and driving a polished Mercedes. He works with four other lawyers in a boutique firm and has an extensive staff supporting him.

Sean takes good care of his body, working out early in the mornings, five days a week. He works out at his local country club where others enjoy his joking and easiness. Sean has reasonably healthy eating habits and limits his alcohol consumption to his expensive vacations.

If he drinks during the workweek, it is only the finest wines that he orders out of the "special" back rooms of fine restaurants. Sean does struggle with sleep problems and his physician has prescribed medication to help the problem. Sometimes his sleep problems cause him to feel mentally detached during mediations or client interviews.

Sean's family belongs to a local house of worship where he serves on the board. He is occasionally asked to give a speech at a church workshop on a legal topic and he does so with great personality and humor. Sean aligns himself with a religious affiliation but does not have meaningful connectedness with a higher power or any spiritual practice at all. Once while he was sitting on the veranda of a five-star hotel in an exotic location, he was unable to sleep and watched a sunrise over a beautiful ocean; he felt a stirring he could not identify.

When Sean is meeting with his clients he is always "present." He listens intently to their stories and offers both professional and personal observations that assist them in moving forward. He has quite a bit of tolerance for hearing their hearts and views his role as an attorney and counselor at law, within reason. Sean tries to satisfy the client and accomplish their goals, even if they are different from his goals. Sometimes his clients get restless working solely with his legal assistants, but when they do have time with Sean, he is so engaged and empathetic that they forgive him. They walk away knowing they have truly hired their knight in shining armor. Sean is also exceptionally diligent about returning client calls in a timely manner. He has been known to call clients a few months after their case closes just to see how they are doing.

Sean's practice continues to grow. He never turns down a paying customer, even when he feels he is too busy. Sean will get up at the crack of dawn to get to the office to do what needs to be done. Although he doesn't enjoy trial work, he will do it if the case requires so. His clients pay a hefty price for trial. Sean is an excellent trial lawyer and always prepared. He is a favorite at the courthouse, always taking time for the court administration staff and judicial gatekeepers to ask about their families and to hear the latest courthouse gossip.

Sean has a beautiful stay-at-home wife and a picture perfect family with three young children. He and his family attend all of the social functions in town and have tickets to all of the events among the "see and be seen" crowd. This provides him with access to all of the wealthiest people in town and his client base consists of many professionals who are equipped to pay top dollar for excellent legal services. At the local yoga studio, his wife has been heard to say, "My husband is the best lawyer in town." His dedication to his family is stalwart even though he often feels held hostage by the social demands on his calendar.

In addition to social events, Sean takes vacations to exotic locations. When he does this it requires juggling of his court and mediation calendar. He leaves this job to his assistant who is well liked by the legal community. He is generous with his assistant and provides her with many bonuses and perks. Even with paying her one of the top salaries in town, the profit she is making for him is tremendous.

Lawyers of all ages like Sean. They work hard for him on his bar committees. If any of them call him with a legal question he will take the time to answer. Sean has spoken at the local law school about the keys to becoming a successful lawyer. Sean does not take an active role in mentoring young lawyers, although he has an open door policy with a startup lawyer renting space in the office next door.

Sean volunteers to head the bar committee in his designated practice area. As the leader he is able to orchestrate the committee's efforts, but he doesn't have to do any of the work of the committee. The judges and bar association applaud him for taking the time in his leadership role. Sean also accepts a solid number of pro bono assignments from the Volunteer Lawyers Program. Each year he is recognized at the dinner for his contributions to pro bono.

Sean's office is in a renovated mansion in the "artsy" part of town. His motto is "keep overhead low" to enhance his profit margin. Sean's fees are some of the steepest in town. He often makes fee agreements with clients whereby he does not provide an itemized billing statement but instead quotes a flat fee for representation. He still reserves the right to renegotiate the agreement if the case goes beyond his anticipated projections of time involved. His fee agreement, signed in every case, provides for fluidity so he can use his judgment in requiring increased fees if a matter gets more complex than anticipated.

Sean embraces innovation in the legal profession. When a new trend or theory is launched, he is among the first to become educated about it. He strives to stay current and engaged in the evolution of the practice. He is happiest in traditional legal practice, but is willing to use alternative practice modalities when they are called for. However, Sean is not a champion of any innovation and doesn't take the time to think about the future of the profession.

So where does the Generous Lawyer stand with the seven criteria for compassionate lawyering?

1. **Compassion for self**
   The lawyer tries to take good care of him or herself and enjoys exercise that involves a group or connection. He or she eats good food, but not particularly in tune with nourishment of body or soul. The Generous lawyer may have a religious affiliation largely for the connection it brings with others, but no real connection to practice of spirituality or solitude. His or her sleep may be problematic.

2. **Care and empathy**
   The lawyer cares for clients but only allows "counseling" to be part of "attorney and counselor at law" in limited segments. He or she may delegate much of the day-to-day work to paralegals or junior associates who are quite profitable. If clients are "needy," the Generous lawyer doesn't hesitate to get more retainer or to value bill for that function. He or she is always prompt in returning client calls.

3. **Respectful**

   The lawyer is very well recognized and well liked in the legal community, as public image is very important. He or she always recognizes and inquires about support staff at office and at work. The Generous lawyer is dedicated to family and engaged with raising children, even if it means getting up before sunrise to get to the office in order to make the soccer game.

4. **Empowers other lawyers**

   The lawyer is an expert at networking and has the ability to put lawyers in touch with other lawyers that can help them. He or she doesn't do a lot of individual mentoring, but has an open door policy. The Generous lawyer may speak at law student meetings to encourage young lawyers.

5. **Philanthropy with the law**

   The lawyer provides public service by sharing their lawyering skills. The Generous lawyer is active in philanthropy events, such as speaking at a law school class. He or she may chair committees in the bar to exert leadership and gain recognition among colleagues and the community. The lawyer may use support staff to handle pro bono cases, but rarely meets directly with the client.

6. **Fair and just**

   The lawyer is clearly profit driven and rarely gives away legal work. He or she charges high prices, but provides quality work. In turn, he or she is known as the lawyer who handles clients with big money. The Generous lawyer prefers not to bill hourly and many fee agreements are for value billing or project based billing.

7. **Legacy for the future**

   The lawyer enjoys being on the cutting edge of law practice and joins committees to be sure they have a presence. The Generous lawyer likes to know about the newest trends in legal practice. He or she does not have a real commitment for legacy to the law due to interest in financial legacy for family.

Pros and cons of generous-style lawyering

Pros:

1. The Generous lawyer takes good care of him or herself, living a relatively healthy lifestyle to stay energized and fit. The lawyer may be lacking in the "spirit" part of mind/body/spirit dynamic. The Generous lawyer operates in integrity, providing a strong sense of peace.

2. Since he or she is much loved by clients, the Generous lawyer gets referrals from former clients and even from opposing parties.

3. The Generous lawyer treats his or her staff well by providing good salary and benefits packages. He or she has support staff that can keep the office running even when the lawyer is not there.

4. The Generous lawyer is recognized as a good lawyer and a "go to" person for other lawyers, which also feeds his or her need for connection.

5. Has a strong public image that can be used for causes that matter to him or her. The lawyer may serve on boards of nonprofits, provide legal service for free or reduced prices, or may advise on legal matters alone or with outside counsel.

6. The lawyer is financially successful, providing a nice lifestyle for self and family. Because of the "value added" of bedside manner and the responsiveness of staff, he or

she can charge flat fees and higher hourly rates than many lawyers.

7. The Generous lawyer keeps abreast of innovation in the law and is often asked to put his or her name as an imprimatur on progressive initiatives at the court, the bar association, or the law school.

Cons:

1. The lawyer takes client or colleague complaints or disparagements very deeply and personally. His or her good feelings about self stem from being accepted by others. As a "pleaser", the lawyer may have stress in juggling demands of family, work, and community. If the Generous lawyer is not working, he or she is likely dealing with family requests and requirements; therefore, may never have time for that deep inner self or creative outlets.

2. Tends to take on too much work, justifying that staff will manage it, but when his or her attention is required, workload may be stressful and burdensome. The lawyer has a difficult time turning away clients who are willing to pay the higher than average prices and who could benefit from his or her legal expertise and bedside manner.

3. If not careful, may cross boundary into gossip as an offshoot of his or her connectedness.

4. The Generous lawyer may be too busy to have a formal mentoring program with younger lawyers who could benefit from his or her expertise.

5. Because strongly profit driven, may err on charging higher fees where clients don't complain. He or she may also be tempted to overcharge because the caliber of his or her clients doesn't have a lot of scrutiny about their legal bills.

6. Because of social concerns and high profile appearance in the community, this lawyer believes philanthropy time and money must be spent on non-legal related causes. This precludes the Generous Lawyer from using his or her unique legal expertise on pro bono cases and other legally related endeavors. If the lawyer takes on a philanthropy role, he or she may delegate the work to support staff.

7. The Generous lawyer is unable to take time to dream or to be creative. As a result, the profession misses out on his or her insights and potential creativity for ideas and initiatives that could positively impact the future of the law.

Profile #3: The benevolent lawyer

Lisa is an attractive, well-dressed, high-energy lawyer. Among all the women in her medium-sized firm, she is the only woman partner/ shareholder. Both Lisa and the firm have a good reputation among colleagues and the community at large.

Lisa takes excellent care of herself. She has become particularly mindful about self-care since she entered recovery for alcoholism three years ago. She was always a functional alcoholic, but after she went through a difficult divorce she sought treatment for alcoholism and overuse of prescription medication. Lisa is now an active member of Alcoholics Anonymous. Since beginning her treatment, she has also increased her physical activity by training for marathons and triath- lons. She enjoys the competitive nature as well as the fact they help her stay connected to her body.

As a single mom to two adolescent children, Lisa shares parenting time with her ex-husband on a week-off/week-on rotation. She is not affiliated with any religious or spiritual practice, but occasionally at- tends the big church down the street from her house because she believes it is important to introduce her children to a faith community. Attending church also provides her access to potential clients. Lisa un- derstands the concept of "higher power" in her recovery, but chooses instead to do a lot of self-talk to calm her down through her stress. She also just goes for a long run when things get too tense.

Grateful for her nanny, Lisa works long hours and has a "Type A" perfectionism in everything she does. She is happiest when others commend her work, clients fawn over her for the outcome she has accomplished, or colleagues simply admire the new technology she has had installed for the office. She is loved by her friends and children, but views their recognition and support as an "automatic" that is not earned and that is not as gratifying as the recognition she gets for her self efforts. Lisa can't imagine being anything but a lawyer.

Lisa's clients are mostly small business owners, so much of her work is transactional and establishing business entities. She is particularly passionate about helping young entrepreneurs get their start and she gives her clients a lot of time, some billable and some not billable. Even when a client is handed off to another partner for their specific expertise, such as intellectual property or securities, Lisa will make sure to check in with the lawyer and the client throughout the process, even if she is not specifically working on the case. Many clients feel that Lisa is an integral part of their growth and success, giving her recognition and credit publicly for her exceptional work. Lisa enjoys the notoriety this brings to her.

Lisa is one of the firm's primary rainmakers. Many of her clients have social and political connections and Lisa cultivates those who are well connected. She is also trying to attract some higher profile clients to the firm, including some startup companies that have bright futures. Lisa speaks on a radio program weekly and takes a great deal of pride in the notoriety it gives her and the firm.

Lisa's goal is to increase the size of the firm. Although her partners are supportive of this, they are not interested in that aspect of the business – they don't like the idea of having to dig into their pockets to come up with additional capital. Lisa oversees much of the administration of the firm, hiring and firing staff, and working with outside vendors on issues such as technology support. She is respectful with everyone she comes across and may even "smooge" to get extra connections for herself and her clients.

Lisa doesn't get to the courthouse much due to the volume of transactional work she does, as well as her high settlement rates as a result of mediation and skilled negotiation. Lisa is very respectful to the judges. She makes sure they know who she is and that she intends to run for the judicial selection committee in her state. Lisa always attends a swearing in of a new judge and makes it a point to circulate around the courthouse when she is there in order to get as much "face time" as she can. Lisa doesn't like to be outdone in court, and takes every adverse outcome seriously and personally. She never compliments or empowers other lawyers and would never offer a job to a good lawyer who had been victorious against her in court, despite her goal to build the firm.

Lisa likes sharing her knowledge with younger lawyers and teaches a transactional class at the local law school once a year. She enjoys doing this so she can seek out the best and the brightest for potential hire as she builds the firm. She will take the younger up-and-coming lawyers to coffee to encourage them, and to be sure she gets the cream of the crop when recruitment comes.

Charitable giving is viewed by Lisa as 'the right thing to do" and she is generous with donations to the local animal shelter and also to the Sierra Club. These causes were picked because she loves to hike and she also has a standard poodle. She has no time to do legal volunteer work or pro bono, although she also sponsors a golf hole at the Legal Aid golf tournament, allowing her to get a sign displayed on the hole with the firm's name. She does require each associate in her firm to do 10 hours of pro bono work per year.

Lisa's billable rates are mid-range and she believes she will always make enough money if she continues to service clients with high quality. She monitors the billing rates and hours of young associates closely, supervising their bills and marking them down when necessary to more accurately reflect the learning curve and the appropriate billing style of a firm, such as hers. When she works with young associates or law clerks to train them on the job, she does not "double bill" the client for both her own and the other lawyer's hourly rate. Occasionally she will take a client at a lower hourly rate, particularly if she believes that client is a feeder for increased business.

Lisa would like to set up a transactional law clinic at the local law school. She believes that legal education can be enhanced. She likes the idea of having her name on the clinic and being recognized for her contribution. She is also interested in using technology to advise clients and often has video-conferencing for consultations. She has also set up some client webinars that have been well received.

Let's see how someone like Lisa, a Benevolent Lawyer, does with the seven criteria for compassionate lawyering:

1. **Compassion for self**
   The Benevolent lawyer may be too driven, leading to over performance in areas of self-care, such as exercise and diet. He or she may struggle with addiction issues or may be in recovery. The lawyer's spiritual life may be lacking or poorly defined, leading to an incomplete sense of self and driving the need for outward recognition.

2. **Care and empathy**
   The Benevolent lawyer cares for clients, but gives more attention to clients that bring them satisfaction and recognition. He or she is active in the firm or company that is in the process of continuous improvement and often interested in efficiency. If the Benevolent lawyer cannot care for a client's needs, they are certain to have a staff person respond in a timely manner.

3. **Respectful**
   Although he or she cares for others, the lawyer may neglect family because of work. The Benevolent lawyer feels more appreciated by helping clients than in being

close with family members. He or she aspires to be well liked by everyone in the legal community and treats others with respect.

4. **Empowers other lawyers**
   The lawyer invests in other lawyers, but mostly those who have a direct impact on his or her bottom line or sense of accomplishment. He or she may speak at continuing education seminars or a law school lecture to try to impart knowledge to younger lawyers.

5. **Philanthropy with the law**
   Philanthropy may involve his or her legal skills or knowledge, but also have strong recognition for them personally in the legal or general community. The Benevolent lawyer's gift giving includes organizations dear to them and may also involve some legal causes.

6. **Fair and just**
   The Benevolent lawyer doesn't overbill but also doesn't give away legal services. He or she has often identified efficiency measures for billing clients so that every effort is captured. The lawyer has a strong fee agreement that is explained to every client.

7. **Legacy for the future**
   The Benevolent lawyer believes that mentoring lawyers in his or her direct sphere of influence leads to quality young lawyers. He or she may invest in efforts at the local law school or legal agency to try to innovate, particularly if they get recognition for doing so.

Pros and cons of benevolent-style lawyering

Pros:

1. Benevolent lawyers are often meticulous and high achieving. They can accomplish many tasks and projects

at a time. Lawyers like Lisa often enjoy their job as a lawyer. While others complain, these lawyers are happy and can't imagine doing anything else.

2. These lawyers are more dedicated to clients than profit. They are willing to go the extra mile for client care and service, even if it is not billable time.

3. Often a high profile person in the community, this lawyer may have power inside and outside the firm.

4. These lawyers are more "plugged in" to younger lawyers and law students, often providing informal mentoring or coaching.

5. Benevolent lawyers give back to charities, especially when they are also recognized for doing so. They may use their legal skills in philanthropic endeavors and typically have some pro bono or low cost clients.

6. The Benevolent lawyer charges fairly and does not "pad" bills or add on extra charges for non-lawyer time or technology.

7. Because of their commitment to service, benevolent lawyers may be innovative, particularly in areas of technology or law office efficiency.

Cons:

1. A lack of balance in high achievement may lead to substance abuse, depression or other physical or emotional challenges. This lawyer may have an insecurity or fear at the root of self, but it is masked by outward achievement and accolade. Continual achievement, accomplishment and accumulation can lead to an emptiness caused by a "never enough" syndrome.

2. Care for clients makes the benevolent lawyer feel important and needed, resulting in self-fulfillment.

3. A single focus may result in missing important family or life events that are irreplaceable, and divorce or tension in family may be an issue. The lawyer's recognition in professional life may be excessive and take a toll on personal life.

4. Although the Benevolent lawyer has the gift of influence over younger lawyers and law students, he or she may not give enough time to mentoring to make a meaningful impact.

5. Philanthropic efforts are most often made when recognition or self-advancement is present, minimizing the possibility for additional effort that could be made anonymously or without fanfare.

6. To be liked and needed by others, the lawyer may give away too much time on non-billable efforts, instead of striking a healthy balance.

7. May not be "awake" to problems in their legal environment or the law in general, causing them to continue in focusing myopically on their imminent efficiency improvements only, without using creativity or innovation to help move the profession forward.

Profile #4: The compassionate lawyer

Every morning Marie begins her day waking very early and making a steamy cup of coffee. Then she spends a period of time in meditation, quietly reflecting on her day ahead. She eats a healthy breakfast and packs a healthy lunch of whole foods and other snacks to take to the office with her. Marie, in an effort to keep her morning calm and quiet, keeps technology off until she is about to leave for the office. She is mindful of her sleep and makes it a point to get an average of eight hours per night.

If the weather is nice and time permits, Marie might take a morning walk after breakfast. If she is not able to get out in the morning or if the weather is bad, she will jump on the treadmill after work and watch the evening news. She tries to make time for exercise at least five days a week.

Marie regularly attends a place of worship where she volunteers to be a greeter. She tries to attend a study sometime during the week, where she learns more about her faith. Marie strongly believes that personal growth, including a spiritual component, is a major part of the meaning of life.

Marie works in a firm with two friends, Mark and Liz. The firm is a general practice firm and has a diverse clientele. Marie makes sure to manage her calendar so she has plenty of time to meet and talk to clients. However, she is tempted to take all the clients she can and struggles with the idea that she has to turn down clients to ensure adequate attention for her current clients. Over time, Marie has learned there will always be enough work when it's needed, as long as she stays true to her commitment of bringing caring, quality work to her clients. If her clients need her, Marie is prompt to return their calls and to make time to see them, even if she has to accommodate them after hours. She tries to keep a reasonable schedule of 8:00 a.m. to 5:30 p.m., but at least once or twice a week she will take a late appointment to accommodate a client. She tries to work only one Saturday a month.

Each lawyer in Marie's firm takes a sabbatical for one full week, twice a year. Every year, for two days, the three lawyers meet at an offsite location as a firm to set goals and measure progress in their work. The remaining time is spent either together or apart, with other friends or family. For at least one of the days of their sabbatical, each lawyer goes alone, without technology and with an ample amount of solitude, doing things they enjoy.

All three lawyers at the firm are dedicated to their clients. When they are with clients, they listen intently. If they have been unable to effectively connect with clients over a period because of scheduling demands, they may set up an in-person or Skype conference to catch the client up on developments in their case. They take the time to carefully explain all aspects of the client's case, including things that may seem obvious. The lawyers return calls, as well as emails, within 48 hours of receiving them. Recently, when a client lost her husband, the three lawyers attended the husband's funeral together.

Marie, Mark and Liz are well liked by colleagues and the community as a whole. While other lawyers may gossip about their colleagues, regularly, the three compassionate lawyers do not initiate or engage in gossip. Instead, they are supportive of colleagues and commend those who may prevail in a court action or who have another accomplishment. Lawyers seek out and confide in Marie in particular, when they are facing professional or personal challenges. Marie always makes herself available for this endeavor. The three attorneys have "go to" attorneys for cases that require a bigger firm's resources and they don't delay in transitioning or partnering with those lawyers.

As a service to their law school, all three lawyers take on one student as a mentor every year. The lawyers make sure that student shadows them in court, during mediation or client interviews, and answers questions about the practice. Marie will often send food "care packages" to her student when he or she is studying for the bar exam. She also stays in touch with students she has previously mentored. Recently, one mentee started his own practice in a small rural community and Marie keeps in touch as he struggles to learn how to practice law, often answering his questions or sending him forms. She has also given speeches to the young lawyers division of her local bar association on topics related to beginning a law practice.

Mark, Marie's partner, writes articles for the bar journal and coaches a mock trial team. Liz does intake at the local Legal Aid office once a month, identifying clients who qualify financially, but cannot be served by Legal Aid. She works to transition a few of those cases to the firm to be handled by Mark, Marie, or herself as pro bono. The firm takes a limited number of low paying clients, discounting the hourly rate and allowing payment plans. The firm is mindful of the clients they take under this arrangement and the lawyers do not take on more than the predetermined number of clients in this category.

Marie, Mark and Liz strive to eliminate wasteful hours on client's cases. They voluntarily turn over requested documents without the need for formal discovery, if the documents fall into the discoverable categories. They use technology efficiently and effectively, and may Skype clients rather than simply call them, if that is available. Their billing program is understandable and they spell out the full charges in express detail on a client's bill. When software licenses are due for renewal, they pay the full and expressed price for the usage, rather than using expired versions without paying for updates. They honestly register each user; they do not allow each other to use the license purchased by only one of them, unless the software contract permits it.

The three attorneys started a "compassionate lawyers society," involving a dozen lawyers who aspire to practice with compassion. The group holds each other accountable professionally and personally, with an aspiration that each will live and lead well. The society also has a philanthropy where they go into a middle school in a troubled neighborhood and mediate disputes. One lawyer goes each week, spending an afternoon with the students, so each lawyer volunteers a half-day each 12 weeks. When one of the students Marie became acquainted with got into some legal trouble, she assisted the student's court-appointed attorney in legal research. Marie, Mark, and Liz are guiding another group of four attorneys who are interested in setting up a compassionate lawyer society as well. They have also sponsored a continuing legal education seminar on lawyer self-care, inviting a psychologist that specializes in stress management to speak and organize the event. They donated the proceeds from their seminar to the Legal Aid Society.

The Compassionate Lawyer when measured against the seven criteria:

1. **Compassion for self**

   The Compassionate lawyer is on a personal journey to become his or her highest self. This lawyer has healthy boundaries, setting limits on the calendar and workload. He or she eats healthy foods, gets good sleep, and has a regular exercise regime. The lawyer also has a spiritual practice in the form of prayer, meditation, solitude or a regular gratitude practice.

2. **Care and empathy**

   The Compassionate lawyer cares for clients and wants to see clients heal and grow, finding joy in this endeavor. He or she may view themselves as a conduit for information and power that creates healing for clients. The lawyer looks for something good in clients and listens with empathy as his or her clients share stories and problems.

3. **Respectful**

   Compassionate lawyers treat all parties in a legal matter and the court, with respect and dignity, despite the behavior of the parties in conflict, but without jeopardizing their own client's position or interest. The lawyer acts firmly and wisely without embittering or embarrassing others. The Compassionate lawyer honors loved ones by managing his or her schedule to allow for time with family.

4. **Empowers other lawyers**

   The Compassionate lawyer empowers other lawyers to serve with compassion and mentors younger lawyers, treats colleagues with respect and dignity, and treats the role of the lawyer as a high minded professional calling.

5. **Philanthropy with legal skills**

   This lawyer provides public service by sharing their lawyering skills. He or she may do this through pro bono legal work, teaching, doing intake calls (triage) at a legal aid office, speaking or writing on legal issues in the community, or providing legal information to people who may not have access otherwise.

6. **Fair and just**
Compassionate lawyers provide legal services at a fair cost, billing clients fairly for services rendered. He or she has a clear manner of explaining fees and charges to clients.

7. **Legacy for the future**
Creativity and innovation in the practice of law is a passion for Compassionate Lawyers. The lawyer uses his or her wisdom and expertise in developing new initiatives, programs, and continuing legal education programs. Compassionate lawyers take appropriate risks in developing legal practices to stay current and fresh in the wake of societal changes and developments.

Pros and cons of compassionate-style lawyering

Pros:

1. Compassionate lawyers maintain a healthy mind, body, spirit lifestyle so they can function at high energy without burnout. They also have a deep sense of meaning and purpose.

2. These lawyers make substantial differences in their clients' lives by modeling calm problem solving to clients who may be poor problem solvers or may be stuck in a victim mentality. The quality of legal work provided is high, and client satisfaction for Compassionate lawyers is at the top of the charts.

3. Compassionate lawyers are respectful of each other and themselves resulting in gratifying relationships with colleagues, the judiciary, and their families. They are leaders in their communities.

4. By mentoring and providing internships to younger lawyers, Compassionate lawyers demonstrate an optimal way of practicing law so newer lawyers are more satisfied in the practice and have a longer tenure as lawyers without burning out or plateauing.

5. These lawyers provide access to justice for clients who might not otherwise have the opportunity for legal representation. They are able to use their legal skills for many different initiatives, enhancing the respect for lawyers in their communities.

6. Compassionate lawyers develop opportunities for innovation in the legal profession, providing exhilaration for themselves and the people they affect through their initiatives.

Cons:

1. Self-care requires consistency, discipline, and time. It may be easier to establish a compassionate practice as a solo or small firm attorney. It can be more challenging to practice self-care in the large firm or in house corporate environment because of productivity demands.

2. Compassionate lawyers often deal with the deep problems and stories of clients, so they are immersed in sadness from all levels of the client's life, which can be draining.

3. These lawyers are in the trenches with other lawyers who may have more aggressive practice styles. Being involved with aggressive or less compassionate lawyers can be stressful, especially when required to practice in a manner that is not authentic. Compassionate lawyers may take barbs from lawyers who deem them and their style of practice as "less than."

4. Investing in other lawyers may require hours of dedication

which may become problematic if strong boundaries are not established.

5. Compassionate lawyers are often "givers" and may see opportunity to give of themselves, beyond what is healthy or reasonable. Again, inability or failure to set appropriate boundaries can cause Compassionate lawyers tend to be overworked.

6. Because the Compassionate lawyer actively chooses to have a full life of balance and health, financial remuneration may be less than with other types of practices. This is also impacted by the lawyer's commitment to using varied fee arrangements to provide increased access to legal services to potential clients.

7. Innovation in the law can be a lonely path. Many lawyers are content with the status quo and have shut down their ability to dream and create. Legal innovators need support from other like-minded lawyers.

Have We Lost Our Way?

When my Dad was practicing law, he would periodically meet other lawyers at the end of the work day for a scotch to discuss a case, and a deal would be scratched out on the back of a cocktail napkin. He would come home for dinner most nights, and spend time with my brothers, my mother and me. He operated a lot like I remember thinking Perry Mason worked as I watched that famous lawyer on television.

What I know for certain is that he drove his practice from a base of compassion.

Are lawyers suffering?

Any of us who live outside our value systems, suffer. Even if we choose to numb ourselves to this reality, there are symptoms that plague us.

If my hypothesis is right, and lawyers are operating in their *deferential* mode and not their *preferred* mode, then like any legal theory there should be evidence that lawyers are suffering with that tension. Let's see what the evidence shows about lawyers today.

Lawyers rank fourth in suicides by profession

According to the Centers for Disease Control and Prevention, lawyers rank fourth behind dentists, pharmacists and physicians in rate of suicide compared to all other occupations in one study.[1]

In 2004 in Oklahoma, there was one lawyer suicide per month.[2] In South Carolina, there were six lawyer suicides within the 18 months before July, 2010.[3] The state of Kentucky had fifteen known lawyer suicides between 2010 and 2014.[4]

What is the source of this? Speculation is that the pressures of the profession including intense financial strains, pressure to bill hours, competition, the perfectionist drive to win every case, dealing with toxic clients, and finding jobs in a difficult economy can be factors. Although every suicide has multiple factors, most experts agree that depression and stress are often key root causes.[5]

Lawyers are 3.6 times more likely to suffer from depression than non-lawyers and the problem begins in law school [6]

Law students may not know what they are getting themselves into when they sign on for a legal education. Two-thirds of Oregon lawyers reported they hadn't had exposure to a lawyer's daily practice before law school and 30% said if they could do it over they would have picked another profession.[7]

Studies show that depression for lawyers clearly begins in law school. Before they enter law school students have the same levels of psychological distress as the general public.[8] In fact some law students report higher levels of positive affect and life satisfaction than undergraduates.[9] But six months after starting law school psychological distress increases dramatically for law students.[10] Although one could argue all professional schooling causes distress, the research shows that compared to medical students, law students have much higher levels of stress, stress symptoms, and alcohol abuse.[11]

Psychological distress doesn't lessen after the traumatic first year of law school. In fact, student stress levels appear to increase as the student continues.[12] One study found that more than 30% of law students are depressed by the time they graduate, while another found that 44% of law students meet the criteria for clinically significant levels of psychological distress.[13]

Getting out of law school and into active practice doesn't help. The levels of depression and anxiety are still significantly elevated two years after graduation.[14]

Reaching out for help can be seen as a sign of weakness

Law school, and the practice of law, prides itself on survival of the fittest. A sense of shame may permeate an admission of feeling over-whelmed or an acknowledgement of inadequacy. One law student I talked to referenced a "mediocre" LSAT entrance test score and the impact it has had on her law school journey. "Every time I want to speak up in class I remember that LSAT score number, and it makes me feel like I am not smart enough to speak up." Admitting this to me was a great act of courage for this student, but telling such fears to professors or other students is rarely done.

When a law school graduate applies for admission to the state bar, there is a character and fitness evaluation. Candidates are petrified that they may put down something that bars their entrance to the practice of law. If they have not been treated for depression, there is no need to disclose it since there is no formal diagnosis. If they do mention it, they fear they will be disqualified from being admitted to practice law.

Even to those that want to reach out, there are few resources readily available. In law school, few campuses have on-site counseling in the law school.[15] The founder of the blog "Lawyers with Depression" (www.lawyerswithdepression.com), tells of going to a law school at the invitation of a well meaning Dean to give a 15 minute talk on depression.[16] He was on the program with others who suffered with stress, alcohol and drug abuse and depression in a program called "mental health." He left feeling forlorn that there had been no tie-in for the students and after the short presentation it was back to the grind.

Lawyers work in confidentiality. They are ethically unable to tell the secrets of their clients under most circumstances. As they carry these confidences, they have no place to unload them. Lawyer support groups are non existent. Lawyers can't even confide in family members about client matters. Most lawyers would also agree that it is risky or even unethical to convey these matters to their own therapists, pastors or priests. Instead, they must carry them or find ways to "turn them over" to a higher power.

For practicing attorneys, lawyers assistance programs have been developed in most states. The American Bar Association formed the Commission on Lawyer Assistance Programs (CoLAP).[17] The group's website points out that during times of "career and financial uncertainty" depression can increase.[18] But what happens to those who do reach out? Most lawyers probably don't know if there are reporting requirements or other ways the well-intended could have an effect on their practices. For many it is safer to live in the shadows with the depression or stress challenges. This is particularly true in this time of firm layoffs and fewer jobs.

Lawyers can suffer from workaholism

Working (and thus billing) long hours is a badge of honor in the legal profession. Most lawyers would not recognize excessive work as an addiction. Instead it is a source of pride.

Beginning with the rigor of law school, students burn the midnight oil out-briefing, out-studying, out-outlining, and out-gunning their fellow students, to the accolades of their professors. When law students walk into their first job they may be told that to be successful they must meet billable hour quotas, and they should be "seen" at the firm on weekends to demonstrate their commitment.

The ABA reports that in 2001 the average lawyer work week was 60 hours per week and that a 40-hour workweek was considered part-time work.[19] In 2007, 56% of "extreme workers" including lawyers worked 70 hours a week or more, 25% worked 80 hours a week and 9% worked more than 100 hours a week.[20]

Joy and accomplishment in the law is often measured by winning a case, which may mean excessive preparation and leaving no stone unturned. Family life may suffer from neglect and result in divorce or alienation from children. Vacations get cancelled due to work. And winning brings in new cases, resulting in increased workload and thus the cycle continues.

Lawyers' propensities for obsessive compulsiveness/perfectionism and competitiveness feed the problem. Tensions from overwork may cause conflict but lawyers are at home in conflict and may not recognize its devastating effect on their personal lives before it is too late.

One lawyer, Steve Angel, bravely shared his story in the Oklahoma Bar Association publication.[21] After he spiraled downward from workaholism that led to major depression, he resigned from the bar. However, resigning actually made his problems worse because of his feeling of complete failure resulting in his becoming a virtual hermit hiding in his house.

Lawyers are the second most likely profession to have a car crash [22]

This is an odd statistic. One study showed lawyers have 106 accidents per 1,000 drivers, second only to doctors who had 109 accidents per 1,000 drivers.[23] There is speculation that this comes from the fact that both professions put in long, grueling hours that result in fatigue by the time they get behind the wheel.[24]

Substance abuse

Studies show about 20% of lawyers have drinking problems, and lawyers are twice as addicted to alcohol or other drugs as the rest of the population.[25] In one sample of practicing lawyers, researchers found that 70% were likely to develop alcohol related problems over the course of their lifetime, compared to just 13.7% of the general population; of these same lawyers, 20% to 35% were "clinically distressed," as opposed to only 2% of the general population.[26]

Alcoholism or chemical dependency is the biggest source of lawyer disciplinary actions in the United States. Law students report more alcohol and drug use than college and high school graduates of the same age, and their alcohol use increases between their second and third year of law school.[27] Another survey found that 11.7% of law students had abused alcohol since enrolling in law school.[28]

Compassion fatigue

Compassion fatigue is defined as "the cumulative physical, emotional and psychological effects of being continually exposed to traumatic stories or events when working in a helping capacity."[29] Symptoms include sleep disturbance, anxiety, intrusive thoughts, a sense of futility or pessimism about people, lethargy, isolation and irritability.[30]

Lawyers often ignore the fact that the work they do impacts them. However a study found that compared to mental health providers and social workers, attorneys had "significantly higher levels of secondary traumatic stress and burnout."[31] Those lawyers or judges working in criminal or family law are considered to be of the highest risk of suffering from this fatigue.[32]

Although mental health workers are in tune with this phenomenon and receive education on the topic, most lawyers have never even heard of the phrase. Those who do prosecution or work for the public defender often go from one long difficult courtroom trial to another without downtime to refuel.

Studies show that the extent of caseload and exposure to people's trauma were the main indicators of whether the lawyer would suffer from this malady.[33] Factors such as years on the job, age, office size, gender and personal history of trauma had no significant impact on compassion fatigue levels.[34]

Technology has impacted the practice

Technology has been a blessing and a curse to a lawyer. While we are able to complete our work more quickly we are also expected to have quick responses to client inquiries and to courts. Taking time to reflect on an appropriate response to counsel on the other side of a case is a luxury that can't always be afforded.

With the advent of electronic filing, lawyers now do much of their interface with the court from a cubicle and a scanner. Gone are the days that lawyers gathered at the courthouse with a sense of collegiality and support. Even judges sit behind a queue putting out orders without the benefit of a lawyer making a personal statement regarding the client's matter. We are all robotic, scanning in proposed orders that are filed with artificial category headings. We no longer show up at the courthouse to convey our heartfelt passion for our client's cause to a judge we hope would scrawl his/her name on the document in agreement with us.

Championing the client's cause no matter what

Few attorneys have the luxury of representing only the clients they believe in, or those with only a righteous cause. Attorneys may have to passionately argue causes that are counter to the attorney's own convictions or moral beliefs.

Further, the lawyer has to fight for the client, in an adversarial manner constantly pushing back every opposing move from the other lawyer. As pointed out by attorney Yvette Hourigan of the Kentucky Lawyer's Assistance Program, "Being a physician has stress. However, when the surgeon goes into the surgical suite to perform his surgery, they don't send another physician in to try to kill the patient. You know, they're all on the same team trying to do one job. In the legal profession, adversity is the name of our game." [35]

Pessimism rules

In the practice of law, one is trained to look at all the horrible outcomes and possibilities that could befall a client. We are to look for flaws in legal arguments and to be critical and skeptical when we hear an argument or position.

57

When a lawyer sits at their desk billing 1600 hours a year or more under this paradigm, it makes it hard to turn into a joyful optimist when we are off duty. This negativity can risk flowing into our personal lives, and impacting our families.

How does the public perceive lawyers?

Recently, a friend in another state had to hire a lawyer to assist her with a legal predicament involving her son. When I asked her how she found her lawyer, she said she got the name from her hairdresser.

I was intrigued that even though she knew I was a lawyer (granted in another state), and one of our mutual acquaintances in her state is a lawyer, she felt compelled to make this very important decision after consulting with her stylist. It made me realize that people who need legal assistance trust the people who have compassion, listen to them, empathize and make connection with them.

In my Dad's law practicing years it was the lawyer you went to first for ANY problem. Today it is apparently the hairdresser.

Apparently my friend is not alone in being wary of lawyers.

The American Bar Association Section of Litigation did a consumer research poll on the Public Perceptions of Lawyers.[36] Roughly half the participants polled had hired a lawyer in the five years before the poll was taken.

While some found lawyers were "well educated, intelligent, hard working, aggressive, outgoing, well spoken and confident," others had problems with lawyers.[37]

Of those polled, 69% said they feel that lawyers are more interested in making money than serving their clients [38]

"I think most of them come out of school with the right intentions, but they figure out, if I do a little bit here and there, I can make enough money to drive a Mercedes Benz" – from a poll participant.[39]

In fact, of all the complaints, the way lawyers charge and account for their fees is by far and away the biggest source of discontent.[40] "My neighbor is going through a divorce. She said that the divorce attorney is charging per hour, and she could not believe how expensive it's getting. She and her husband are trying to work things out as far as what to do to avoid all these hours." – from a poll participant.[41]

Of those polled, 73% believe lawyers manipulate both the system and the truth [42]

"I think they manipulate the law. Well, that's part of the job, to interpret, and I guess manipulate is the kind of perception we have" – from a poll participant.[43]

Clients polled told stories of personal injury lawyers that "hooked them up" with a doctor who was in cahoots with the lawyer to give a favorable medical report.[44]

As I write this, a friend's daughter is involved in a lawsuit for an automobile accident that was not her fault. The lawyer she selected has sent her to doctors and physical therapy for what were minor injuries and as a lawyer I know her lawyer is building the file.

Her mother noticed that while she was previously healing nicely, now that there is a medical protocol hanging over her it has negatively impacted both her mood and healing. I had offered to call the insurer on her behalf before extensive treatment to get a fair reimbursement but she declined because of the promises the lawyer she sought out made about bigger dollars if she got extended treatment. Essentially, we taught her to use the system. Interestingly the lawyers get blamed when it's the consumer who goes along with the plan. We are TEACHING people to abuse the system.

Consumers in the poll were also dismayed at the way we police ourselves [45]

Only 26% of those polled agreed that "the legal profession does a good job of disciplining lawyers."[46] One has to ask why only lawyers sit on many ethics committees. Would it be helpful for our profession to have more laypersons providing input on how lawyers operate? Arguably, such input would help us be more consumer aware in our practices. Apparently continuous process improvement, a strong concept in the business world, is not of importance to lawyers.

Those polled also were distressed about lawyers who take on cases they are not equipped to handle, lawyers who are incompetent and lawyers who promise what they cannot deliver [47]

I am always interested in clients who come to see me for a "second opinion." When I give them my legal opinion they will mention the promises made by another lawyer. Upon further inquiry I ask them whether they are PROMISES or POSSIBILITIES.

I have come to learn of an interesting phenomenon. There are lawyers who PROMISE results. Then, when they don't get the result, they blame the judge. Again, what are we doing to instill confidence in lawyers and our system in general with this approach?

Those polled weren't terribly concerned with the fact lawyers DO advertise.[48] They were more concerned with the tenor of the ads. Their problems came when the ads seemed to imply a lawyer could get guaranteed results.

Complaints about lawyers weren't limited to just one type of lawyer [49]

Here are some of the themes of discontent that those polled registered about types of lawyers:

Criminal defense lawyers: represent guilty clients

Prosecutors: cut too many deals

Public defenders: inexperienced and over-extended

Personal injury lawyers: chase ambulances and pursue frivolous cases

Divorce lawyers: exacerbating conflict

Corporate lawyers: engaging in underhanded practices in the interest of their clients

Were there any lawyers who had a positive reputation in the poll? Yes! Real estate lawyers who are viewed largely as functionaries, and civil rights lawyers who are viewed as working in the public interest.

In another poll, 44% of those polled indicated that ethics displayed by television lawyers are better than real world lawyers. They also felt 51% of lawsuits filed are frivolous/unnecessary.[50]

We are strategically positioned to heal and influence

The poll referenced above also found that the general public believes lawyers have the power to make a real difference.[51] This impact is not only for those individual clients but for society as a whole.

I believe the possibilities are even greater. Lawyers, once we move to compassion, have a chance to help heal the world.

A friend's daughter worked at a daycare for a time. One of the first rules she was taught by the corporation was that they could not hug or cuddle a child. My first instinct was that daycares most likely initi-ated the rules because of lawsuits and lawyers. As a working mother, I always felt slightly guilty about having my children in daycare. How sad that nobody could hug or cuddle them when I could not.

Lawyers have been responsible for profound positive changes in civil rights and other important matters. When we get behind such issues as same sex marriage, anti-discrimination policies, free speech and other value driven matters, we persuade the nation to change its course. We have brought important issues to the forefront such as access for people with disabilities. As a result of our work there is more disclosure when things are being bought and sold. The lawyers who are put on the court as judges have influence in legal outcomes that change the trajectory of people's lives.

Lawyers are strategically placed in people's lives at the time people are most wounded, vulnerable and distressed. They have lost jobs, personal injuries, fractured families, troubled children, broken contracts, houses in foreclosure, work injuries, business failures, debt overload, possible jail sentences and most any other type of life devastation one can imagine. At these moments we have more access to clients than even their physicians, because we are dealing with their hearts and souls.

As lawyers, we possess tools as a result of our education, our experience, our own life stories, our confidence and our ability to communicate. Who better to be there, at that very critical moment in a wounded person's life?

When clients come to us they are vulnerable. Things that happen at the initial contact and throughout a relationship with a lawyer can have lasting impact and can change a person's life course or even their destiny. What we do MATTERS DEEPLY.

Can our own malaise, and society's opinion of us change if we operate from a sense of compassion?

If so, how do we move toward compassion?

Moving Toward Compassion

As I was writing this book, there was a part of me that knew my message would be controversial. Old wounds of feeling "less than" popped up, eerily similar to those I had in law school.

I told a lawyer friend of mine about the book and she replied, "Sounds interesting but don't make it too fluffy." When I mentioned it to another colleague, he assumed I was writing for family lawyers and small or solo firms, but not the "big firms." I was struck how the very mention of compassion seemed to imply a softness or weakness that is not befitting of lawyers.

I searched for the meaning of the word "compassion." I found that it is usually defined as the sense of having a deep awareness of the suffering of another, accompanied by a strong desire to alleviate the suffering. I started to reflect on whether lawyers could, or even should, operate from a foundation of compassion.

As I continued to worry about delivering my message, I felt an overwhelming desire to go to my Greek Orthodox Church for the liturgy, although I had not been there for quite some time. During the liturgy, the Bishop was visiting from Chicago and the service was elaborate. Eventually, the Bishop settled in to give his homily, based on Luke 10:25-37.[1] "At that time the lawyer stood up to put Jesus to the test…" My heart started to race as he continued to read the only Bible passage I know of containing the words "lawyer" and "compassion." It was the story of the Good Samaritan.

It begins with a lawyer asking Jesus what he needed to do in order to inherit eternal life. In response, Jesus asked, "What is written in the law? How does it read to you?" The lawyer, in response, quotes Jesus' teaching of loving one's "neighbor" as oneself. Jesus replies that the lawyer had answered correctly. Instead of requesting further instruction, the lawyer asked, "Who is my neighbor?"

Jesus began telling the lawyer a story of a man who was robbed, stripped, and beaten, then left for dead. A priest came upon the man and noticed his suffering, but passed by on the other side. A Levite also saw the man, but also passed on the other side. Then, a certain journeying Samaritan came upon him. When the Samaritan saw the man, "he had compassion, and came to him, and bandaged up his wounds, pouring oil and wine on them; and he put him on his own beast, and brought him to an inn, and took care of him." He then left money for the suffering man. Jesus ordered the lawyer to love his neighbors as the Samaritan loved the suffering man.

The Greek word for compassion used in this passage is ἐσπλαγχνίσθη. The definition literally means "the inward parts, especially the nobler entrails – the heart, lungs, liver, and kidneys."[2] In the story above, as written in the original Greek, the Samaritan had compassion in the Greek meaning – a deep, heartfelt emotion that goes all the way down to your guts. Unlike the Latin term for compassion, "compatior," which means "co-suffering," the Greek meaning goes even deeper.

To be a compassionate lawyer is to act with compassion, as it is described in the story of the Good Samaritan. To my colleagues, compassion isn't fluffy. It is gut-wrenching.

We are privileged to have one of life's highest callings.

Compassionate lawyers recognize their power and influence

Lawyers are among the few professionals that have an impact on every person and every aspect of society. We are positioned in the most influential aspects of our society, such as politics, government, the judiciary, public policy, and education. We are positioned in the most vulnerable levels of society including prisons, mental health hospitals, amidst the physically wounded and the overburdened workers. We work with all of these constituencies as "The Lawyer."

Even in our personal lives, once we are distinguished as a lawyer, we have incredible influence. People whom we encounter at a coffee shop, the gym, the homeowner's meeting, or our place of worship, whether directly impacted by our work or not, label us as "so and so the lawyer." Thereafter, they watch us closely.

The compassionate lawyer recognizes that lawyers are leaders and you don't take off your lawyer hat when you leave the office. You are a lawyer even if you don't practice law. Justly or unjustly, once a lawyer, you are branded with the label.

In recognizing our power and influence, we must be aware that results are not the only way we are measured. While results are noble goals for lawyers, even a court victory may destruct and overwhelm the client. For example, while a lawyer may have the ability to obtain the homestead for a client in a divorce, the client may not be capable of making the mortgage payments. In turn, the client is left with financial disaster and further problems; the end result actually harmed the client. Likewise, a person fired from a job may get reinstatement as a result of our intervention, but they may suffer from self-defeat and depression once back on the job. Compassion must be one's primary objective; the proper results will follow.

Compassionate lawyers recognize that the people we touch are suffering

Some who visit a lawyer are visibly suffering. They may reveal physical wounds and describe the pain from a traffic accident. They may show mountains of credit card statements and a notice of foreclosure as they inquire about filing bankruptcy. They may be shackled or handcuffed as we meet with them regarding criminal charges. They may come to us because they stand to lose their house, children, pension, spouse and dignity due to divorce. In turn, we as lawyers must respect the courage and vulnerability of those we work for and with.

Having been the client in my own legal action when I divorced, I have a renewed sense of recognition that the people I touch are suffering. I cringe at the thought of my lawyer using my story, my life's deepest pain, as the fodder of lunchtime revelry. It may be difficult to recognize suffering, however, if we do not share the client's experience.

Compassionate lawyers must be sensitive in order to understand one's suffering. This process takes patience. Imagine your brother or sister, child, best friend, or even your loved one sitting across from you telling the story the client is telling. Would your outlook on the matter be different?

In the book and movie, *"A Time to Kill,"* authored by a lawyer, John Grisham, a young black girl was murdered. The defense lawyer, played by Matthew McConaughy, delivers a compelling closing argument. He describes the murder to the southern jury, slowly and intensely painting the graphics. As the argument comes to an end, he delivers the most powerful line stating, "Now imagine she's white."[3] Instantly, the white members of the jury can relate to the matter; they also experience the suffering.

Compassionate lawyers recognize that with suffering, comes negative energies

In his book *"Power vs. Force,"* David Hawkins, MD, reports his study on the measurement of emotions.[4] The study measured the power emotions had on the physiological body and determined the calibration of various emotional states. The results were that the emotions which created life-enhancing energy were, in ascending order: neutrality, willingness, acceptance, reason, love, joy, peace and enlightenment.[5]

Conversely, Hawkins found those emotions that were life-draining and thus created substantial body weakness were, in descending order:

pride, anger, desire, fear, grief, apathy, guilt and the most toxic emotion of all: shame.[6]

Where do the emotions of those who are seeking a lawyer calibrate?
Not likely at the highest calibrating energies of enlightenment, peace,
joy and love. Rather, they are often stuck in the four lowest level emotions. Shame is the front-runner and according to Hawkins, shame is
life draining.[7]

Dr. Brené Brown defines shame as "the intensely painful feeling or
experience of believing we are flawed and therefore unworthy of love
and belonging."[8] This is a straightforward description of the clients I
see in my law and mediation practice. Although many are what would
be deemed "high conflict," at the root, they are often floating in shame.
As lawyers, we interact with people experiencing shame on a regular
basis; however, few of us recognize it.

Furthermore, experts in restorative justice and restorative practices
also agree that shame greatly affects one's quality of life. Donald
Nathanson, former director of the Silvan S. Tomkins Institute reports
shame is identified as a critical regulator of human social behavior.[9]
Nathanson identified four reactive behaviors associated with shame,
including withdrawal, attack self, avoidance, and attack others.[10] The
most frightening part of his research is the determination that "[the]
attack other response to shame is responsible for the proliferation of
violence in modern life."[11] In other words, one's shame leads to blame
or attacking others, and blaming another leads to conflict.

In law school, however, we are trained to blame and attack the other
once the client begins his or her story. The lawyer immediately starts
thinking of who to blame and how to develop a legal cause of action
against that person or entity. It is no wonder the "attack other response"
proliferates violence. Everyone blames everyone else, and does so at
the hand of his or her skilled marksman, the lawyer. We must do our
best to shift clients from shame to higher calibrating energies; blame
is not the answer. In fact, according to Dr. Hawkins, courage is where
power first appears.[12] When clients move to courage, it becomes a
level of empowerment for them.

Compassionate lawyers provide a safe environment for people to become vulnerable in sharing their suffering

In a time of need, people seek someone to listen to their story, whether it is a family member, friend, priest or rabbi, or counselor. Our clients come to us after deciding they need to tell their story to a lawyer. They decide the best person to sit with them in the dark of their hurt and pain is a person with a law degree. These people, at their lower moments in life, make themselves vulnerable to a lawyer. It is daunting yet exhilarating to realize the power we have as a profession. What we do matters deeply.

The first contact with a client sets the tone for not only the attorney-client relationship, but for the client's impression of lawyers as an entire profession. Now, reflect on lawyers you know. Are they ones who leave a good impression of the legal profession, especially when considering compassion?

Lawyers have power brains that are powered up, multi-tasking at any given moment. From our first day in law school, we are taught to simultaneously identify issues, relate them to real causes of actions, find hidden scintillating pieces of detail that become evidence, and then file everything away in a vast array of subcategories to prove every element of a cause of action.

However, our power brains can have a tremendous effect on our ability to provide a safe environment for the vulnerable. First, it diminishes our ability to be fully alert to a client's story if we are not focusing solely on his or her telling. It is impossible to effectively listen with an open heart if we have not turned down the volume of other matters running through our head. We must be confidential, focused, and most of all, compassionate with our clients.

Compassionate lawyers are on the front lines of a person's journey to healing

The first step of healing is to alleviate suffering. Borrowing from the medical profession, healing is not curing. To cure is to successfully control or stop the spread of an illness, or in the legal profession, to aid in the recovery from conflict. Curing does not mean the illness will not recur; on the other hand, healing is when the illness eventually ceases.

Curing usually involves a professional taking charge. For example, a patient may not become engaged in actively fighting disease, but instead simply says, "Just cure me." When the patient is not engaged, however, complete healing is unlikely. This issue directly translates to the legal profession, when a client simply says, "Just take care of my case."

In his book, *"Getting to Resolution,"* attorney Stewart Levine discusses that "[d]elegating conflict resolution to professionals who know how to diagnose and resolve your problems is a culturally learned response. But delegation compromises us when the professionals believe they are experts better equipped to make the key decisions that affect the core of our lives. Conflicts are filled with our feelings, and the professional to whom we hand the conflict does not have to live with the results of the resolutions."[13]

If we as lawyers do not engage our clients in their own matter, they are less likely to have the ability to heal. Furthermore, Levine emphasizes the importance of client involvement in order to resolve conflict. Standing in the shoes of a client, he says, "[m]ost of us avoid taking personal responsibility for conflict resolution. Even though our culture is litigious, we lack the courage to connect deeply with others and we personally avoid confrontation."[14] Clients hand us their issues – it is our responsibility to carry them along during the resolution process, rather than run with their case. We must allow our client to heal, rather than cure them ourselves. Our focus should be to resolve conflict in a way where the results best reflect the client's desires and move their lives forward.

The first thing we must remember when clients come to our office is do no harm. The most important part of our interaction with people is the moment we sit together to discuss the ailment that brings them to the lawyer. Failing to give enough time, attention, and empathy at this juncture does harm. How we initially respond to them will make or break our path of compassion.

A few years ago, a dear friend called me sobbing. Her mother was slowly dying at a hospice house. She and her brother went to the mother's probate lawyer to discuss the will, knowing death was imminent. The lawyer tried to explain how the estate was set up. My friend, in a whirlwind of grief, did not understand and asked repeated questions. The estate lawyer commented to her, "It's not rocket science!" My friend was shamed in the midst of her pain. This lawyer, strategically placed in this woman's life at a pivotal, vulnerable moment, wounded her. He did harm.

Lawyers who are actively engaged in compassion do no harm, but also recognize opportunities to empower people to take charge of themselves and their lives. Compassionate lawyers bring clarity to chaos and set the stage for the healing energy of compassion, including hope, courage, determination and inner strength.

Clients trust compassionate lawyers with their stories

"When we're looking for compassion, we need someone who is deeply rooted, is able to bend and, most of all, embraces us for our strengths and struggles. We need to honor our struggle by sharing it with someone who has earned the right to hear it. When we're looking for compassion, it's about connecting with the right person at the right time about the right issue," says Brené Brown, a noted researcher[15]

Lawyers have been referred to as "dark sitters," as we sit in the darkest moments with people who are hurting. I have also heard the term "story catchers" because the people we work with have important stories to tell. As the front lines, our reaction to one's story can perpetuate shame or healing. We must give full attention and be empathetic.

When we listen to one's story, our power brains usually skip empathy and move directly to the legal diagnosis. Much like the doctor who hears a story and immediately responds, "You probably have cancer," lawyers may respond, "It's likely you will have to give up primary care of your children and half of your pension is going to be gone." We forget to listen deeply and empathize with the person, even though his or her experience is different than ours.

Research suggests that people with the most social power have little empathy for those with little power.[16] Specifically, "the poor, compared with the wealthy, have keenly attuned interpersonal attention in all directions, in general, those with the most power in society seem to pay particularly little attention to those with the least power."[17]

I will never forget the skinhead Nazi that came to my office for mediation. The man was intimidating, wearing a wife beater t-shirt displaying an assortment of tattoos. His soon-to-be ex-wife, sitting in the next caucus room, was having an affair with a man of another race. The whole atmosphere was intense and I was struggling to figure out how to relate to this person with whom I had nothing in common.

As we introduced ourselves, out of sheer desparation to make a connection, I expressed interest in his body art. For the next several minutes he went through the tattoos showing me all the different hate inspired stories he wore so proudly. At the end he landed at one on the inside of his right arm and said, "This one represents my mom who had ovarian cancer. I crawled in bed with her and held her in this arm when she was dying." In that moment I had empathy for a man I had previously brushed off as a monster. I found myself guilty of being judgmental; I had little empathy until I consciously focused on it.

A compassionate lawyer looks in the mirror

As the parable goes, when each of us looks in the mirror, we see two wolves; one is evil in anger, regret, greed, self-pity, guilt, and self-doubt, while the other is good, full of joy, peace, love, hope, kindness, compassion, and faith. This fight is going on inside each person. With a fight like this, which wolf will win?

71

The one we choose to feed.

So, is what we are feeding ourselves as lawyers what we should be feeding ourselves, as *compassionate* lawyers? Let's find out by looking more deeply into each of the seven standards.

PART II

Chapter 5

Mind, Body, Spirit

Compassionate Lawyers operate from wholeness of mind, body and spirit

MIND: WE MUST BE THE MASTERS OF OUR POWER BRAINS

A compassionate lawyer controls the volume of the power brain; he or she manages work and other commitments, while quieting the noise and eliminating all negative self-talk.

The "power brain" can be both a blessing and a curse. With the amount of data we absorb, it's a wonder anything meaningful can be unearthed. I am in awe of lawyers with the ability to cite statutes and case law like the clergy cites Bible verses.

Intellect is the name of the game for lawyers. But where is wisdom?

Recently, an elderly lawyer came to my office for mediation, mistakenly arriving a half hour early. He lumbered in, bemoaning his age. It was my first mediation of the day, so I welcomed him into the conference room to chat. I listened as he told me about some of his incredible experiences as a lawyer. I was excited to notice how quickly this lawyer, who had only worked with me once before, felt comfortable telling me his story in the quiet of my conference room. His rich stories, full of lessons and experiences, were intriguing to me. I could easily sense his compassion as he mentioned experiences and spoke of his work with clients.

Another colleague of mine recently returned from Afghanistan. He served as a judge advocate general (J.A.G.), where he monitored the military, ensuring we were operating within the rules of war. When he came back home, after having been away from his family and his firm for two years, he was changed. When he transitioned back to the trenches of the lawyer world, he seemed to have a whole wealth of experience that he was keeping inside.

Both of these lawyers stuck out to me because I resonate with them. It goes back to a wound I sustained in law school. I was given the subtle message that intellect was all that mattered; cases in books are all that matter; arguing and advocating is all that matters. Intuition, life experience, inner wisdom, and transformative moments in our own lives are to be minimized and shelved.

How do we reclaim these gems that are essential to our aspirations in transforming into a compassionate lawyer?

Manage the amount of cases, projects, and other commitments you take on

"To allow oneself to be carried away by a multitude of conflicting concerns, to surrender to too many demands, to commit oneself to too many projects, to want to help everyone in everything, is to succumb to violence. More than that, it is cooperation in violence. It destroys the fruitfulness of his own work, because it kills the root of inner wisdom which makes work fruitful." – Thomas Merton[1]

Compassionate lawyers begin the journey of "mind" by reclaiming their inner wisdom, re-wiring their concepts of time, and being compassionate to themselves. It is important to note that being compassionate doesn't mean we don't set boundaries.

At one point in my career, I found myself taking on an overwhelming amount of cases without discernment and was focused on one goal: to "bill the hours." As a result, I had too many clients who weren't motivated to heal or be helped, and I was drained due to their anger and

76

bitterness. It was a losing proposition for all. Although I was making more money, I was also failing my other obligations – I was sloppily managing my personal finances, I had to drop off the parish council of my church, and I was half-heartedly assisting my family members in crisis. I was being pulled in a million directions, but wasn't succeeding in any area. Nothing was fruitful.

Lawyers can fall prey to overwork. With our worth defined by billable hours, we have to work more to bill more. What we fail to realize is the work we do as lawyers is power brain quality. That means that instead of a "regular" hour we are engaging our minds for the entire hour, at full capacity. We might be physically present for hours on end at the office, grabbing the three o'clock cup of coffee to keep chugging, but at some point our mind has to reach overload. If we think we can work 8-10 hours per day of billable time at full kilter brainpower we are fooling ourselves. If we look closely at the quality of work that happens at that over-the-limit phase, we recognize it is sub quality. Then we berate ourselves for lack of perfectionism.

I finally realized this and started setting clear boundaries with my time and energy. Although it was difficult, it was a key to my health and productivity. People got upset with my decision to change things. I stopped volunteering for things, turned down committee work, and started referring cases to other lawyers when I was at capacity. During that transitional time, I had bouts of guilt for the clients I had to turn away, especially when they were referred by other good quality clients. The quality of work I provide today, however, is better than it ever has been. I not only find more joy in my work, but I have more joy and satisfaction in my life in general.

Lawyers, particularly small firm or solo practice lawyers, are at risk of being swayed by the scarcity mentality. The caseload and client base often ebb and flow depending on the time of year. Family lawyers, for instance, often find that work is slower in the summer when families are energized, distracted from drama or chaos. Once the kids go back to school and the routine settles down, the phones light up. This is when a lawyer, coming off a "dry spell," may take on more cases than he or she can handle.

Similarly, personal injury lawyers are living from settlement to settlement, or trial to trial, due to uncertainty in obtaining contingent fees or labor intensive cases. Our work and efforts are not to make us "busy" but to make us "fruitful." Balancing the quality of our work and our ability to be compassionate to others and ourselves is challenging. Until we ratchet down and focus the power brain, we cannot be fruitful.

Quiet the noise

Everyone needs stillness and silence. We need nature and scheduled times of quiet.

A friend of mine sets an alarm on her computer for a few times during the day. At the chime, she sets everything aside for 30 seconds. She relaxes and clears her mind, simultaneously taking a slow, deep breath. At first blush, 30 seconds may sound worthless, but it has been proven that moments after meditating, we not only feel calm and content, but we have a heightened awareness and empathy.[2] Scheduling quiet time regularly "can permanently rewire the brain to raise levels of happiness."[3]

Turning down or off the technology is another step to quieting the mind. The media is everywhere; televisions and magazines are in every gym, restaurant, and waiting room; the Internet is accessible by nearly every phone and laptop. However, the news and social media have a tendency to put off strong negative energy at times. This does not only affect us, but our clients, the wounded. I do not provide a television in my waiting room. It is important that my clients have the opportunity to be reflective before we meet. Although I set out magazines, I am selective, ensuring that negative news is not lingering in my office.

Although I do my part in eliminating technology, it is inevitable that clients are still affected. Photos of new girlfriends/boyfriends, incriminating photographs that have been uploaded, and posts of disparaging comments are now brought into evidence in cases. It is not surprising that studies show one in three people feel worse after checking Facebook, experiencing feelings of loneliness, envy, and dissatisfaction with their own lives.[4]

My solution has been to implement a morning routine. I aspire not to turn on any technology until I am dressed and ready to leave the house for the office – no television, phone, or laptop. I have a quiet morning that may include prayer, exercise, reading uplifting material, taking a walk, making an elaborate breakfast, or sipping coffee in my favorite chair. Depending on the morning, it may involve all of the above! I now have the ability to start every day with my power brain calm, focused, and under control. I am managing it – it is not managing me.

Quieting the negative self-talk

Lawyers appear, to the outside world, to have it all. People perceive us as smart, rich, self-confident, and carefree. My experience with lawyers, however, tells me otherwise. Like all over-achieving perfectionists, we have an intensity that can be problematic. We are in a highly competitive environment where everything is in the public eye and every mistake is magnified, at least in our own mind.

While I was cross-examining a witness in a recent trial, I felt momentum and turned up the heat, doing my best to discredit the witness. My argument involved an exhibit that contained numerous calculations in a spreadsheet. While I was questioning, I realized that the exhibit, the foundation of my argument, was missing an important piece of data. Of course, opposing counsel did not hesitate to point it out. I had a momentary segue into "deer in the headlights." Wouldn't you know it; sitting behind me was my then 26-year-old daughter. It was the first time she had ever seen her mother in action in the courtroom.

I continued with my witnesses seemingly effortlessly, but I was so disappointed and self-deprecating in my head that my effectiveness was momentarily impacted. My daughter critiqued my performance with compliments – to the extent that I was "a really awesome lawyer." At that moment, although it was difficult, I did my best to let the situation go and quiet my negative self-talk.

It is known that women, in particular, are prey to negative self-talk. Even if men only suffer 10% as much, it can be dangerous. As harsh critics of our own self, we can calibrate in shame, doubt, guilt, fear and apathy if we let the negative self-talk prevail. Most of us can talk so lovingly and instill encouragement with our clients, our children, and our friends, but we struggle to do so with ourselves.

It took a long time to extend grace to myself, to brush off mistakes and imperfections, and to constantly remind myself, "I am doing the best I can." Now, through training my mind, I replace those messages with powerful declarations of positivity. I have turned down the volume of the power brain. In turn, I have found peace.

That doesn't mean I am 100% successful in this endeavor. Old habits die hard. Of all the three components of mind, body and spirit, the most difficult one for me to control is the mind. It takes practice and diligence. Becoming aware, and recognizing the unique aspects of our lawyer ways of thinking is a first step.

BODY - WE MUST CONNECT WITH OUR PHYSICAL SELVES

A compassionate lawyer respects and appreciates the body, connecting with his or her physical self by eating clean, properly sleeping, and being active.

Many lawyers are unknowingly disconnected from their bodies. They are focused on work and juggling a busy schedule, all while taking care of family responsibilities. Adding in care of the body is not usually high on the priority list. After an incredible eye-opener, however, I had no choice but to put my health at the top of my list. Before I map out my advice, I want to share my experience.

One Friday evening I was working late when my law office phone rang. It was a former client, a woman physician, who explained that her friend and female colleague was in the middle of a divorce and wanted to change lawyers. We chatted and I agreed to meet the woman, Dr. J,* the following week.

* Dr. Jean Lorentzen, D.O., is an internal medicine physician in West Des Moines, Iowa.

80

Dr. J's lawyer had done a fine job of representing her. It was the lawyer's "bedside manner" that made her seek a change in representation. She felt she needed more compassionate lawyering. I was impressed by Dr. J and her innovative approach to medicine and health. We concluded we could work well together and she transitioned her case to my office.

About six weeks before Dr. J's trial, I took a trip to Northern California to spend time with a friend. I took Dr. J's file with me to work on in my downtime. One day when I was working on the case in my hotel room, I began to feel a horrible heaviness come over me. It was unfamiliar and frightening. It was a feeling of dread, anxiety, panic, depression, sadness, and emotional paralysis all at once. I felt suffocated, so I went out into the fresh California air to breathe. When I went back inside it began to happen all over again. I brushed it off and didn't mention it to my friend. I forgot about it when I flew home and turned my attention back to my busy work schedule.

As Dr. J's trial date approached, my paralegal began to put the documents together. The case was document intensive, so I also had to put in long hours. I was mentally and physically exhausted. I vividly remember being home, in my favorite chair and feeling physically paralyzed from getting up. I was literally stuck to the chair like glue. I burst into tears unable to understand why this was happening.

A few weeks after the trial, I received the judge's ruling and called Dr. J to share it with her. I also found myself asking if I could make an appointment to come to see her professionally.

A few weeks later, I was in Dr. J's office for a physical, answering questions during the initial two-hour consultation. She asked questions I had not been asked by other doctors. Her approach made me feel calm, like she had all the time in the world for me. She questioned my nutrition, sleep, and spirituality. I now realize she is a compassionate doctor.

I did not have good answers for most of the questions she asked. I was hardly sleeping, I skipped meals, often eating microwave popcorn for dinner, and I over-exercised, trying to stay trim and fight stress. I did not have a healthy work/life balance as I spent the vast majority of my time at the office. I confided to her the strange experience I'd had while working on her case.

After she completed the intake, she sat back in her chair and looked me straight in the eyes. "Lawyers are some of the sickest people I treat," she said. "They have so much stress and bad health habits that their bodies are shot. I want to do some blood work, but I have to tell you that based on what you have told me, if you don't change your life soon it is only a matter of time before you end up sick, or worse." I panicked. Had I lawyered myself into disease?

My blood work revealed some reversible irregularities that largely stemmed from my poor choices of over-working, little sleep, and poor nutrition. Dr. J pointed me to a poster in her office. It said the following:

The Dalai Lama, when asked what surprised him most about humanity, said: "Man. Because he sacrifices his health in order to make money. Then he sacrifices money to recuperate his health. And then he is so anxious about the future that he does not enjoy the present; the result being that he does not live in the present or the future; he lives as if he is never going to die, and then dies having never really lived."[5]

She asked me then if I was ready to heal my body. Although the correct answer was obvious, I didn't know how to respond. I worried about having to take on one more project of learning to cook, figuring out menus and worst of all, packing a lunch. Her urgency was sincere and I knew I would do it. As we discussed earlier, some close the book when "journey" or "self-healing" is mentioned. I knew I had no choice but to begin my journey to heal my body.

Of course, I wouldn't be much of a lawyer if I didn't remind you – do not take my advice, but check with your own physician. I insist, however, you talk with a compassionate physician. If, of course, you can find one.

Clean up your diet

The body takes in everything we put in it, on it, and around it. At about the same time I embarked on my body-healing mission, my son started working at Whole Foods. He came home telling me the same things Dr. J had. I concluded that if I was getting the same information from both sources in perfect synchronicity, I should be paying attention.

Clean eating is defined as "consuming food in its most natural state, or as close to it as possible. It is not a diet; it's a lifestyle approach to food and its preparation, leading to an improved life – one meal at a time."[6] My clean eating plan consisted of three meals and two to three small snacks, including a lean protein, plenty of fresh fruit and vegetables, and a complex carbohydrate with each meal. This approach keeps the body energized and burning calories efficiently all day long. After years of starving to stay thin, I almost had a guilt associated with eating.

Dr. J warned me that I should not expect to change everything overnight. She analogized, saying, "If an airline pilot is flying to a destination and the instruments are only one degree off, the plane could end up in a far off place. If you change your diet only 1% you will make a huge difference in the way you feel and the quality of your health." She encouraged me to eat two green vegetables every day.

I started out with something revolutionary. I ate a good breakfast, every morning, and stopped skipping meals. Before, I used to dash to the courthouse, grabbing a Starbucks double latte and a high fat muffin or croissant. I started eating eggs or oatmeal, or if I were in a hurry, I'd throw together a protein smoothie. My energy levels were much higher and I didn't get hungry as frequently.

For lunch and dinner, I was accustomed to frozen dinners, if I even ate. Over time, I found that consuming vegetables, particularly my required greens, was measurable and achievable. My refrigerator began looking like a jungle, colorful and leafy. I began to keep healthy options at the office, or if I had a break, I would treat myself to the salad buffet at Whole Foods. I felt great.

Dr. J also made it clear that pop and soda, even diet, was the equivalency of poison. I wasn't a big pop drinker, but I decided to swear it off and stopped offering it to clients, instead serving water or tea. I now shudder when I see people come to mediation with "big gulps." I observe their energy, finding they act tired and agitated.

As I began feeling better, I easily noticed people sitting with me in mediation, depositions, or trial preparation had such low energy. I kept healthy snacks in my office for clients and lawyers during proceedings. I found that by nourishing them with healthy foods, their attitudes improved, rather than making them more lethargic.

A lawyer who often comes to my office for mediation told me one day that he always ate McDonald's for breakfast and he was gaining weight. I jokingly volunteered to be his health coach. On the one percent theory, I suggested he limit his McDonald's breakfasts to two or three times a week and that on other days he might go to a local diner instead. A few weeks later, he was back and requested a coke due to low blood sugar. I didn't have a coke, but I offered him a boiled egg and whole grain crackers. He joked that of all things, he didn't expect to be served a boiled egg at mediation.

He was in my office recently after I hadn't seen him for a few months. He reported that he had followed my suggestion to cut down on the McDonalds breakfasts. He started cooking breakfast at home and eliminated pop. In turn, he was down 15 pounds and has managed his low blood sugar. As I spoke with him, I could sense his boost of self-esteem and energy. Just the initial 1% change spurred him on to a healthier lifestyle. I was so happy for him.

Because we put in long days, and often work around the clock when we have a deadline lawyers use caffeine. I remember well the gross coffee machines in law school. I am amazed at the lawyers that are in my office for afternoon mediation and ask for a pot of coffee at 4 p.m. Now the younger lawyers can mainline caffeine even better though energy drinks.

I was in trial a short time ago, and the opposing counsel sent her client's father to a local drugstore to purchase her a five hour energy drink. She told the judge she needed it for her health and asked if her client's father returned after court was back in session if she could ask for a two minute break to drink it! I had a nutritious bar in my brief-case and wanted to offer it to her, but I knew she equated caffeine for energy instead of nutritious vitamin enriched bars.

The problem with caffeine is that it is a quick fix and doesn't solve the underlying problem of having poor nutrition and spikes and valleys of blood sugar, as we skip meals and grab whatever we can find in the office kitchen. As we drink more caffeine, we become tolerant and need more and more of it much like a drug. It is also a diuretic so it depletes our body of necessary hydration. While there is nothing more satisfying than a hot cup of coffee, to use it as a crutch to keep us overworking further disconnects us from our bodies.

I realized early on that I had a sugar problem. I love sweets, hearkening back to my grandmother's house and the infamous candy drawer she kept just at child height. We could go there and have whatever we wanted. As I look back now I see that my grandfather developed adult onset diabetes and I wonder whether the candy drawer was partially responsible.

Dr. J's admonishment to eat only "real" foods and to look for hidden sugars ultimately led me to begin to read labels. I found sugar every-where, including in breads and other foods that you'd least suspect. More interesting was the fact that the sugars were usually manufac-tured and not even the real thing. That meant the more sugars I ate the more I wanted to eat because they weren't filling me with any nutrition.

I turned to fruits, and bought a Vitamix blender. I started making smoothies throwing strange things into them like romaine lettuce and blueberries, among other ingredients. I'd pack a green and fruit smoothie to take to the office and sip it throughout the day, and after dinner I'd have a bowl of fresh berries. I even started an "apple a day" crusade never having known there were so many different types of apples.

Of course, chocolate had to stay. However, I decided if I was going to have chocolate it would be the best chocolate. I found that dark chocolate with blueberries and other similarly decadent chocolate bars were nirvana, and if I really needed it instead of picking up some cheap sugary candy at the convenience store I kept my chocolates like fine wines and savored the taste.

Improve your sleep

Lawyers are sleep deprived from the moment we begin law school. Whether it is perfecting an appellate brief, preparing for trial, or staying awake stressing over work, we are notoriously poor sleepers.

When I saw Dr. J, I was hardly sleeping. When I did sleep, however, it was fitful and I woke up several times per night. Many nights I was working files or trying cases in my sleep. Dr. J prescribed Epsom salt baths and magnesium supplments. I had heard of Epsom salt baths, and I started taking them regularly. Sadly, it took me awhile to even allow myself to slow down to sit in a bathtub. My life, as with most lawyers, moves at record speed. Once I allowed myself to slow down, I felt fantastic. Judith Orloff, M.D. found the same oasis:

"My tub is my refuge after a busy day: it washes away everything from bus exhaust to long hours of air travel, to personal unpleasantness. While you relax, water works on you. It has alchemical cleansing properties which will purify your physical body and energy field."[7]

While I took my prescribed baths, I would consciously leave behind all the emotional and stressful clutter of the day and relax. Before going to sleep I would take two Calcium-Magnesium pills (220 mg of each mineral) that Dr. J had me pick up over the counter. I also removed the television from my bedroom and read until I fell asleep. My sleep improved significantly.

According to Phil Gehrman, PHD, when you don't get enough sleep, cortisol, the stress hormone, is released rather than somatotropin, the growth hormone.[8] Studies show numerous health effects of insomnia or limited sleep including depression, impairment of reasoning, heart disease, lowered libido, and weight gain.[9] Another study compared brain imaging of sleep-deprived and rested individuals, and studied what those individuals were eating.[10] The brains that were sleep deprived responded more strongly to fatty and sweet foods.[11] The mind-body connection is woven together through the magic elixir of sleep.

Some may say, "I am a person who doesn't need much sleep." I was one of those people. A sleep researcher, Matthew Walker, says, "I think you have about 16 hours of optimal functioning before the brain needs to go offline and sleep."[12] Once I started getting eight hours of restful sleep, I showed up at the office, clear headed and rested and feeling prepared to handle anything. My sleeping improvement, paired with clean eating, has allowed me to deliver at my maximum ability. I can administer compassion in a way that is life enhancing rather than life draining.

Move your body

Former President John F. Kennedy said, "Physical fitness is not only one of the most important keys to a healthy body, it is the basis of dynamic and creative intellectual activity."[13] Accommodating an exercise program into the schedule may seem like one more burden, but it is truly the third leg of the "body" formula.

Brain researcher, John J. Ratey, M.D., emphasizes the impact of exercise on one's mental issues, including stress, anxiety, depression, attention deficit, and addiction.[14] According to Ratey, "toxic levels of stress erode the connections between the billions of nerve cells in the brain" and "chronic depression shrinks certain areas of the brain."[15] In his book, Ratey tells of a time he was cross-examined in a case about whether the woman patient was managing her anxiety through exercise.[16] He describes that "I launched into a twenty minute monologue about what exercise does for the brain."[17] I suspect that he got away with a monologue on cross because the judge and lawyers were interested in his topic while wondering if they could apply it to their own lives.

For most of us, beginning to do anything physical is good. Walking, whether done on a treadmill or outside, is touted as the best exercise to begin a workout program. Some lawyers' daily exercise consists of going back and forth, from their desk to the restroom. Others may be weekend warriors, spending hours at the gym on Saturday and Sunday, and then resuming a sedentary lifestyle during the week. We should aim for the middle of the spectrum. Although some believe that "more is better," we need to start simply doing something most days of the week.

My journey of being active was a less difficult adjustment. I have run half marathons and finished 100-mile bike rides. I explored many areas of fitness; from being an obsessive "spinner" and attending body pump classes, to lifting with personal trainers. Among all, yoga has been my constant and provides me the most overall benefit. I find there is nothing else that makes me feel quite as serene and fit as yoga. The best part about that I don't need a gym – I can roll out my mat and do a few minutes of yoga first thing in the morning.

According to Ratey, "The point I've tried to make – that exercise is the single most powerful tool you have to optimize your brain function – is based on evidence I've gathered from hundreds and hundreds of research papers, most of them published only within the past decade."[18] The more connected I have become with my body, the more I realize the importance of physical activity. Even when eating and sleeping well, I don't calibrate as highly if I go more than a day or two from physical activity.

SPIRIT: OUR HIGHEST WORK COMES FROM CONNECTION WITH SPIRIT

A compassionate lawyer connects with the spirit, practicing gratitude and forgiveness.

The term "spirit" can be controversial because it is often associated with religion. Once religion is discussed, everyone takes notice and prepares to debate. Spirit, however, is not religion. As a compassionate lawyer, you will find where the concept of spirit fits in, and you don't have to explain, argue, or justify it to anyone. While I share my ideas in connecting with spirit, I offer an open invitation for you to take what is meaningful, add what you want, remove what doesn't serve, and formulate your own design. This part of the journey is the most personal and beautiful part of a compassionate lawyer's foundation.

One definition of spirit is "the part of you drawn to hope." Caroline Myss, author of "*Anatomy of the Spirit*," expands the definition, describing it as "The part of you seeking meaning and purpose... the part of you drawn to hope... that has to believe in goodness or something more."[19] In Greek, Spirit is πνεῦμα pronounced "Pnevma," which is also the word for "breath."[20] Spirit literally means the breath of God. In times of great stress, I remind myself to simply breathe, and by doing so, I am connecting with Spirit. We weave our spirits into everyone we meet and everything we do.

As mentioned, a journey of spirit does not necessarily mean one is religious, although it certainly could. I have found great satisfaction in my own religion, but my world of spirit is not confined to my religion. To me, the world of spirit involves an awareness of everything around me.

Accessing the spirit

It is believed that spirit guides our life path. When we find ourselves in a position to betray our integrity, our wellbeing, or ourselves, it is usually because we have taken a detour from where our spirit is directing us. In my early days of law school, I was betraying myself by trying to formulate into the lawyer I thought I was "supposed" to be. I heard my inner voice warning me, but I kept going. I zoned out my intuitive guidance and took the detour.

Spirit creates a longing, and if we aren't attentive to the call, we tend to fill it with the wrong things. Some choose to fill it with alcohol, drugs, or even more work. As lawyers, if we don't practice authentically and compassionately, we may feel uneasiness within. My own journey of "spirit" has allowed me to guiltlessly follow my path, and in turn, I have been directed to compassionate lawyering.

As I traveled the lawyer's spiritual road to compassion, I realized that every choice I made in my personal life, as well as my work life, either fed or depleted my spirit. Over time, it was apparent that my work life needed the most spiritual guidance. In assessing the situation, I knew I needed a method to help me reconcile my clients' suffering, so I turned to the foundational source for my own spiritual world: prayer.

I try to keep my heart vigilant as a lawyer and mediator. My early morning quiet time is important for the fortification of my spirit. I often sit in the silence and seek spiritual direction for which people or families, including my clients, have issues that weigh particularly heavily on my heart. Then, I write out a prayer for them.

A heart of gratitude

Spirit emanates from the heart. It is often believed that the heart is the center of the value system. Evidence of a grateful heart may include a positive attitude, awareness of God's presence, a humble spirit, peacefulness, thoughtfulness of others, generosity, unselfishness, expression, friendliness, contagious attitude, motivation, a servant's spirit, fruitfulness and joy.

The practice of gratitude is another factor in assessing the Spirit. When I remind myself, daily, of my blessings in life, I find that I am more grounded when I am face-to-face with clients. When I was recovering from my painful divorce, I would try to write out five things I was grateful for, even if it was the same five, or a variation for a few days in a row. I have found that when I express gratitude and focus on the spirit in a meaningful way, my heart is full. In fact, a study has shown that when people made an effort to take note and recognize things they were grateful for, their happiness in life increased while depressive symptoms decreased.[21]

As far as my law practice, the most rewarding part of focusing on spirit is that it has given me absolute freedom to follow my heart and be authentic. I no longer feel I have to "play with the big boys" in order to be validated as a lawyer. Instead, I can interact with my clients in a way that suits me. I may hug clients when they need comfort, pray with them in a time of need, or cry with them in a moment of sadness.

A previous client of mine would occasionally come by unexpectedly at the end of the day for weeks during his case. We would sit and talk about his distress, then follow up with small talk. I would listen intently for 15 minutes, free of charge, and he would leave feeling better. Not only do my clients benefit from my style of practice, but I also feel rewarded at the end of the day. Even though there are plenty of rough days as a lawyer, there are many if not most days that the work and the people you meet are exhilarating. Gratitude for being a lawyer is high on my list.

Creativity

Compassionate lawyers can enrich their spiritual journeys by exercising their mind creatively, whether it is writing, painting, listening to music or something else. In the book, *"The Creative Lawyer,"* lawyer author Michael F. Melcher emphasizes that as lawyers, we are trained to be "issue spotters" who identify potential problems and "take things apart, look for flaws, compare possibilities against evidence, contemplate problems, see cracks in arguments and contemplate risks."[22]

However, this can lead to an unfulfilling career as a lawyer because finding fulfillment in the legal profession requires "breaking things down into discrete, actionable chunks and doing rather than thinking."[23] Melcher suggests in order to avoid living a life that is a day-to-day grind, we should all take 20 minutes each day to reflect and strategically plan our day. By mixing in an awareness of spirit with creative thinking, it can lead us to an internal satisfaction and compassion for others and ourselves.

I have always loved writing. As part of my efforts to exercise my spiritual mind, I started attending writing workshops at the University of Iowa Writer's Workshop, blogging, and writing this book, *"The Compassionate Lawyer."* It feeds my soul.

There are many ways to access spirit and embark on a spiritual path. To be a compassionate lawyer you have to take the first step and recognize it is a journey. Once you have found your spiritual place, you must continue to stay "plugged in." Similar to mind and body renewal, it is easy to fall out of the habit of nurturing spirit unless you hold yourself accountable.

Each day I leave my house, I stop at an icon of Christ on my wall. I bow my head and say the following prayer by Marianne Williamson: Where would you have me go? What would you have me do? What would you have me say, and to whom?

Managing difficult emotions

Buddhist monk Pema Chodron has said, "Working on ourselves and becoming more conscious about our own minds and emotions may be the only way for us to find solutions that address the welfare of all beings and the survival of the Earth itself."[24]

We mentioned how lawyers often have to operate in our deferential styles, rather than our authentic styles. As a result of this incongruence, we can become emotional without even realizing what is causing it. I had this happen in a case I took to trial.

My case involved teen parents and the fight over parenting time. I represented the teen mother. As I was cross-examining the teen father, I found myself getting more and more aggressive. Twice the judge had to tell me to "dial it down." When we broke for lunch I spent time alone in the empty courtroom wondering what in the world had overtaken me that I had to be quite so "over the top."

As I was driving home from the courthouse at the end of the trial I thought of my work as a mediator. I started to dream about the type of resolution of the case that I might have assisted in crafting in a mediation setting with two compassionate lawyers involved. The outcomes were based on similar cases I have mediated and were not beyond the realm of possibility.

Instead, my client and her family were left dissatisfied noting that they felt in the courtroom like they were "just another case" to the judge. It reminded me how closely our clients study the judge to see if she/ he is listening or interested in their case. I am sure our judge was listening and interested and he asked very good questions of his own after the examination by lawyers. I was pleased with the judge's well-reasoned ruling in light of the facts and evidence. Yet the clients felt empty in the process.

The sadness that came over me, despite a job well done, was over-whelming. While the judge's ruling took care of the problem, it did nothing to heal the family. In fact, as in many trials, my own "mud slinging" made matters worse. And most of all, I seemed to be able to easily abandon the compassionate lawyer and turn into some type of barracuda at the flip of a switch.

The next morning I got a call from a client, the wife in a collaborative divorce case. She was bemoaning that her husband, who was being cooperative, was in agreement on the settlement terms but could not get a call back from his collaborative lawyer. The husband got on the phone with his wife and started to complain about his lawyer. I was in a difficult position because I did not want to throw my colleague under the bus and I didn't want to cross a boundary by having communications with the other client without the other lawyer present or on the phone.

When we hung up I texted the lawyer's private cell number, left voice-mails and did everything I could to get the lawyer's attention, but to no avail. My client and I were both being disrespected by the lawyer and I was livid with anger at my colleague. I realized this was a spill-over from my trial persona and I hadn't totally put that ugly litigator to rest.

Ultimately, I realized that I needed to get control of my emotions before I started to feel comfortable in the deferential mode. In the deferential mode I was likely to do things that were counterintuitive, and being driven by emotion and fatigue.

I moved my schedule around and went to a yoga class. When the instructor told us "leave whatever doesn't serve you behind on the mat" at the end of class I laid down that deferential style and spiritually reconnected to my authenticity and serenity. I went through the rest of the day calmly and peacefully, knowing that I had control of my emotions and could be responsible for only my own actions.

Forgiveness

Another practice involving spirit is forgiveness. Certainly we can all remember things we have done that make us feel empty and full of regret. As overachievers and perfectionists, lawyers tend to hold on to mistakes and every faux pas.

I know that as a young lawyer I would second guess myself on cases, and then agonize after the matter was over as to whether I had been "good enough" in my client representation. Did I get the client a good enough result? Were my efforts good enough? Was I interested enough in my client or had I discounted them as "just another client?"

In some instances the answer was "no." I had made mistakes. I had done a job that could have been done better. I had taken a case to trial that should have been settled. I had settled a case that in retrospect, should have been taken to trial. I had minimized a client's agony.

I will never forget an early family law client that I agonized over for years, feeling I had undersold the client's alimony case. I remember many nights where I worried about whether she would be able to support herself. When I churned cases in my head as I drifted off to sleep, hers was always at the top of the heap.

At least ten years post representation, I was at a cocktail party and ran into my former client. She came toward me and I cringed. She gleefully threw her arms around me and said she wanted me to meet her new husband and they had just gotten back from Hawaii. She told me she would be forever grateful for what I had done for her in the divorce.

This made me realize that there is a "bigger picture" going on with many of our clients. All I can do is the best I can, with my gifts and talents, to help people as best I can. Things I have done that are wrong, deliberate, mistakes and ineptitudes must be released. I have to forgive myself for those lapses in thought, word, and deed on my cases and with my clients. Forgiving others can be difficult but not nearly as difficult as forgiving ourselves.

The journey to mind, body and spirit is a critical piece of becoming a compassionate lawyer. This component accomplishes a foundational piece in becoming whole. When we learn to have compassion for ourselves, we are whole, calibrating at the high levels of peace and joy.

Chapter 6

Caring

Compassionate lawyers have genuine care and empathy for the people they serve

Imagine yourself greeting clients for your first morning meeting after you have enjoyed a relaxing evening, slept well, and you have had a peaceful morning. You are rooted in gratitude and prepared to take on the day.

In this scenario, when we meet our clients and other lawyers, compassionate lawyers are meeting them from a place of high energy. We are calibrating in a life enhancing way. Perhaps we are feeling at least willingness, or maybe even joy. We are prepared to get on the battlefield. In a recent four-way-collaborative meeting with two clients and two lawyers, myself included, the other lawyer exclaimed, "I just got hit in the face with Kim's pom pom." I was taken aback by the comment until I realized he was complimenting my energy. When one calibrates at joy or higher, it is noticeable to a world that is tired and numb. I was unaware that my energy was so noticeable, especially to that lawyer. Once we begin taking care of ourselves, we calibrate higher and notice the energy of those around us. In turn, we are better equipped to care for others, including our clients. Our energy supports us in fine tuning our problem solving skills.

Meet people first as fellow human beings

When we meet our clients, we must first connect with them as a human being and then as an attorney. As mentioned earlier, in law school we are taught to be an attorney the moment anyone begins to tell their situation. However, if we rev up the power brain right away, we may be judgmental, possibly labeling the client as "negligent," "too emotional," or "irrational" from the beginning. Kirkegaard said "Once you label me you negate me."[1]

Before we begin a legal analysis, compassionate lawyers take time to listen to the people in front of us, first tuning in with an open heart and keen attention to what they are saying. We remove any and all barriers that affect our listening, including judgments. Talking to our clients as fellow human beings is to simply recognize they are also on life's journey. We do not have to be in agreement with what they say, but we must understand. Philo of Alexandria said, "Be kind, for everyone you meet is fighting a great battle."[2]

Check your ego

As lawyers, one of our biggest barriers in making an initial connection is our own ego. When we are operating from "ego," we feel that we are defined by what we have, what we do, or what people think about us. We believe we are separate from everybody else and also separate from what's missing in our own lives. Ego has been described as Edging God Out – we edge out all possibilities except what we do and think. When our ego is at the helm we are operating in a state the opposite of compassion.

Ego challenges can start in law school. I will have the law students I teach look around the room on the first day of class and notice that virtually all of their fellow students are exceptional in some way, often intellectually or through accomplishments in their endeavors in high school and college. The students are often driven and competitive, resulting in ego taking a front seat.

Once in practice, lawyers are easily prey to the ego because we have an incredible power to influence. Clients hang on our every word. They may also feel intimidated working with someone they view is "better/ smarter/more successful."

The compassionate lawyer must constantly be checking his or her ego. To keep our ego in check we have to practice humility and benevolence (giving). By greeting clients warmly, talking to them first about ordinary things, and getting a glimpse of who they are, we are taking the chill off the clients' nervousness.

Many lawyers feel the case is the lawyer's case, and not the client's. The lawyer may feel that the client is paying for legal judgment and the client must get in line with the lawyer. There is a delicate balance. In the best situation the lawyer and client are working as a team. But the client's voice and desires need to be the focus of the representation.

Recognize the influence of our own gatekeepers

Compassionate lawyers recognize that our gatekeepers give the first impression of the lawyer. By the time the client is across the desk from a lawyer, he or she has had interaction with either an assistant, or, at a minimum, a voicemail or email inquiry. Are we paying attention to the way our secretaries or assistants handle our incoming inquiries? A good test might be to have a friend call as if they were a client and listen in. Imagine that the person calling has never met with a lawyer before and they are scared. If our staff people are rude, indignant, disinterested or poor listeners, potential clients are likely to view lawyers the same way.

Some lawyers do not return calls of incoming potential clients if they are at their workload capacity or if they screen the message and decide the client seems unworthy of a consultation. Many clients have told me that my office is the only one that responded to their numerous outgoing calls to a number of firms in seeking a lawyer, even when the purpose of my return call was to let them know I wasn't currently taking new clients. When I put myself in the shoes of the frustrated client, I imagine myself as a medical patient with a severe illness. I cannot fathom the fear and anger I would have if not a single doctor called me back in a time of need.

Sometimes we are able to sense that potential clients are not within the purview of our practice, but people in crisis deserve the minimum dignity of a call back. If I am too busy to respond, or if I am not taking new cases, I will forward the inquiries to one of the young lawyers whom I have on a list I keep. Lawyers on that list have agreed they will absolutely call the client back, even if they too believe it is not a good fit. They inform the client that I am not in a position to take their case, but that I asked them to follow up and that they are capable of helping the client.

Be a deep listener

The most difficult skill for compassionate lawyers is one that is also difficult for most human beings. That is, we must listen deeply. If we listen as lawyers first, it is virtually impossible to actually listen as we go through a mental agenda and take lengthy notes, barely making eye contact.

When we sit down to listen to the client, chances are they are about to tell us their story. This moment is the most important for the client. We should make it a point to direct our body toward them, sitting with a strong posture. We should keep a legal pad, but only to write down necessary bullet points, for further discussion with the client. Compassionate lawyers do not interrupt the client or begin giving advice or feedback until the client has finished his or her story. When I was a child, my grandmother Josephine taught me to listen, telling me, "Don't go broadcasting when you should be tuning in."

Learning not to interrupt is perhaps the hardest skill I have had to learn, and I am still challenged by it. Any interruption should be for a brief comment only, such as "That must have been so frightening" or "That must be so painful." Make comments to them, human-to-human, not lawyer-to-client. Clients usually pour out their story and thrive on the safe environment when someone is listening with an open heart.

After hearing and validating the story in "human" mode, we can then pivot into lawyer mode. If we conclude the client is someone we can help, we can set an appointment for follow-up, or sign a fee agreement and begin representation. If he or she does not fall within our practice area, we can refer them to other compassionate lawyers and wish them the best in the future.

Lawyers are well connected. We have the ability to explore and refer clients to other professionals who can help them. Would a call to our close friend, the banker, help them with their lending issues? Could a CPA help them with the ancillary tax issue they alluded to? Would a colleague in juvenile law be able to guide them with their teenager whom they briefly referenced? Sometimes giving them another referral or picking up the phone to make an introduction is all we can do for them. I've often made such calls to others in the middle of a client initial consultation. We must go the extra mile to be a problem-solver.

How can we become better listeners?

1. **Listen for interests.**
   "Interests" is a word that is similar to "needs." Good listeners are attentive to what is below the surface. What is driving the person we are listening to? What emotion or fear is at the source of what we are hearing? As we identify the emotion, need, or fear, we have a basis to direct our comments to the client in a way that resonates with them. When we can tell them how our legal assistance may meet their desires, they are more apt to listen closely to our legal advice.

   As lawyers we are trained to listen until some legal principals emerge, and then we start putting the facts into the elements of a legal cause of action. Once this is identified a lawyer might say, "What you are telling me has elements of tortious interference with contract!" and then we hijack the conversation. Instead, continue to listen before labeling the cause of action.

2. **Maintain eye contact.**

In my mediation training seminars, I often have the attendees partner with someone who they do not know very well. I instruct them that for the next period of time they are to remain still and maintain intense eye contact with the other person, without talking or losing connection. I silently clock 20 seconds. Afterwards, most participants are agitated and feel that the period of time seemed at least a minute long. Most lawyers also feel that making eye contact with clients is uncomfortable.

However, it is true that greater eye contact leads to greater connection. When the lawyer makes eye contact, the client feels he or she has the lawyer's interest. The next time you talk with someone, make it a point to see if they keep eye contact and notice the effect it has on you.

A trainee in one of my recent mediation trainings came back to the class the day after we studied eye contact. She reported she had done an experiment after class the night before. She had gone to Wal-Mart and had made a deliberate point of making eye contact with people she came into contact with. The results were unexpected. Not only did people hold eye contact with her rather than dropping their eyes, she reported that the majority of them smiled warmly at her.

3. **While they are talking, do not compare the client's story to another case.**
Clients' stories can have threads that are similar to other clients' stories. As the client talks, we are likely to be reminded of the other similar case. Instead of comparing the cases, side-by-side, for the duration of the discussion, jot down "Smith case" as a reminder, and then resume listening to the client's story.

4. **Don't appear to be rushed.**

Law may be the only profession where every minute is precisely measured and accounted for. In turn, we are always conscious of the time. However, we must be careful not to fidget or glance at the clock during our conversations with clients. When a client sits down to talk with a lawyer, it is critical that that time is spent uninterrupted and free of distractions.

As a mediator, I am amazed at how many lawyers will text or email on their phones or laptops during the mediation while their client sits next to them and begins pouring his or her heart out to me. Even after I return to the caucus room, having spent time with the other party and attorney, the attorney may still be on the phone regarding another matter, often using other clients' names and leaving the distressed client in the mediation to sit idle. Aside from the ethical issues and the potential breach of confidentiality, it is heartbreaking to see the client left emotionally abandoned by the busy attorney. Needy clients may be draining and to sit with them for long period of time can be unnerving. At a minimum, the lawyer should leave the room for brief spurts to make calls or discuss other cases, or to simply take a break from the intensity of the client. However, a lawyer who abandons the client, leaving him or her alone, is missing a chance for compassionate lawyering. Sometimes the lawyer is truly the only support person for the client.

Can you imagine the fear and anxiety the client may experience while sitting alone in a mediation, which could affect their destiny while their lawyer is on the phone with a different client in an adjacent room?

5. **Validate feelings.**
Feelings are the emotional state or reactions the client expresses as we interact with them. It is helpful to first identify the client's feelings; however, if he or she does

not verbally describe feelings, we can try to imagine how we might feel sitting in the client chair. Then, we can validate that the way he or she feels is understandable, given the circumstances. In doing so, we may say one of the following:

"Thank you for sharing your story. I can understand how frightened you must have been when you saw that car coming toward you."

or

"Losing your job after so many years must have been very painful. I can understand how you felt betrayed by your employer despite all your loyalty."

Even if we think the client is overly dramatic, it is important to realize the anxiousness that comes when telling a painful story to a stranger. Lawyers that have little tolerance for deep listening and validation often believe that "if clients want to talk about feelings and get emotional feedback, they should see a counselor." However, we are called "attorney and counselor at law." Without the counseling component we fail to put the humanness in relationships with our clients. Instead, it distorts our job description in a way that is not compassionate. For some lawyers, the idea of validating a client's feelings may be too frightening because the lawyer has never paid any attention to their own feelings, as they are out of touch with themselves.

6. **Tell clients something that lets them know you understand, but don't try to top their story.**
Sometimes the lawyer may have a life experience of their own that is similar to the client's. Lawyers should not necessarily feel sharing this is "off base," as it may help the client know that the lawyer understands. In this vein,

I have a blog chronicling my own personal divorce journey. Some of my colleagues have criticized me for this, stating I'm too "out there." However, I feel it is helpful for my clients to know even seemingly "perfect" lives can be devastated. This allows me to direct the client to my blog for that information at their leisure without wasting time in our meeting with "my story."

7. **Ask follow up questions.**
   One of the most famous quotes from a classic book, *"The Seven Habits of Highly Effective People"* by Stephen Covey, is to "seek to understand before you can be understood."[3] After you have validated the client's feelings at the conclusion of his or her story, an easy method of seeking clarification is to ask at least three follow-up questions.

   For example, when we hear something that is offensive, before responding, we could ask questions such as:

   - What was surprising to you?
   - How did that make you feel?
   - Does that cause you concern?

   Often, particularly if they are directed to the client's needs and interests, the questions provide clarification and a new insight to what the client is explaining. If the client has shared something overwhelmingly shocking, follow-up questions also give us an opportunity to regroup.

   The magical question, "What would you like to see happen?" seems to provide the most useful information in virtually every scenario. This can help the client begin to brainstorm and identify his or her desired solutions. Whenever I ask this question, I always smile in anxious anticipation of what comes out. From there, I try to direct my comments to determine if and when the resolution stated is achievable.

In one of my skills trainings I took life coaching. The hallmark of the style of coaching I learned is that the person I am coaching has all the wisdom inside of them, if I just guide them through questions to help them unearth that wisdom. I have found this premise to be true with clients as well. By patiently guiding them through questions before advising, I am much more in tune with what they need.

8. **If you must tell the client a war story, make it short and relevant.**
   Lawyers are notorious for telling war stories to our friends, loved ones, and of course, to each other. These stories may be helpful in discussing how the court handled a similarly situated legal matter, or how a client reacted to a similar issue. However, we must be careful that when the client is telling his or her story, we do not interrupt or give feed-back by sharing a war story unless it is short and very relevant.

9. **Allow the client to ask questions first, based on what they think is important.**
   After the client has asked their questions, it's time to give your legal advice. Our clients are paying us for our legal advice, but chances are they have burning questions that matter most to them. At the conclusion of the client's narrative of their story, we may respond to the client in a matter such as, "Thank you for sharing your story with me." We then validate their feelings. Finally we may ask, "Before I begin to give you my thoughts, what particular questions do you have for me?" By asking this question we get to the root of the client's desired information. We can first give advice in direct response to what the client is asking, and then offer to give other feedback based on the perspective of our legal advice.

10. **Don't overpromise results to get the business.**

In our quest to reassure the client, and perhaps land the business, we often overpromise what the legal process can do to fix the client's problem. Compassionate lawyers are honest about what the legal process can and cannot accomplish. Although we have the ability to remedy certain aspects of the client's problem, in most cases, the legal system can't make everything better. As lawyers, we often have the unfortunate duty to tell the client that the legal system can't accomplish their specific desires.

One of the lawyer's biggest stressors is that case results often depend on the determination of a judge, jury, or a prosecutor. Every lawyer who has had trial experience can regale with war stories of when the court "got it wrong" despite our best efforts. Law is not a precise science. However, sitting with clients as they have these stark realizations is some of the most difficult but gratifying work of a compassionate lawyer. If you oversell what you can do, the client is rewounded once the result comes out differently than you led them to believe.

Listen for the lower calibrating emotions

As compassionate lawyers, we must identify lower calibrating emotions. These emotions are pride, anger, desire, fear, grief, apathy, guilt and shame. Once we identify these emotions are in play, we must adapt our listening techniques accordingly.

Shame

The lowest calibrating emotion is shame. The best antidote is to tell the story to someone trustworthy. Brené Brown has provided the following pointers when encountering shame stories.[4]

1. **Don't act shocked or surprised by what they tell you.**
   After practicing law for more than 30 years, I am quite convinced that I have "heard it all." In turn, I find it easier

to maintain composure during a graphic or tragic story. However, for younger lawyers, it takes practice and experience to keep a poker face. Sometimes, clients will warn their lawyer, prefacing the conversation with "this is a very difficult thing to say," or "this is probably one of the worst things you have ever heard." When this happens, I reassure my clients that my office is a safe place to tell their story.

Recently, a woman came to my office, and as soon as the door closed, she exclaimed, "I was sexually assaulted last night when I stopped at a convenience store to buy cigarettes!" I reacted with empathy and calmness rather than shock. She was scheduled to come in prior to the assault for an unrelated matter, but we changed gears to deal with the assault.

2. **Don't blame them or blame the other party.**
When the client has told his or her story, do not put immediate blame on anyone. Instead, you can calmly respond, "I understand. Thank you so much for trusting me and for being so honest about everything." Discussions regarding blame and other legal concepts should be reserved for a later time after the situation has "soaked in" and when you may have to have the difficult conversation about fault from a legal perspective.

3. **Don't minimize.**
I have a client I represented years ago who surfaces every couple of years and calls me "superwoman." She comes to tell me things and asks for my advice. I have found that particularly for women clients, I am often an ongoing resource for them even after the case closes.

Often the things she shares with me are shame based stories that are mostly anxiety and not legally actionable issues. Because I know she trusts me, I take the time to listen to her. When I do, I don't tell her things such as "it's not as bad as you think," or "don't beat yourself up." Instead I listen as a safe harbor for her and try to get her to identify courageous ways she can deal with the issues she has raised.

4. **Don't respond with sympathy rather than empathy.**
   In being sympathetic, the famous line is "I feel so sorry for you." However, sympathy sounds insincere and it is disempowering to clients, as it may allow them to stay in the "victim" mode. Our job as compassionate lawyers is to empower our clients to find courage to heal. Darwin said that sympathy is the greatest instinct for humans. However, sympathy in the legal world can be a good first step to its greater emotion: empathy.

Guilt

Guilt can be defined as feeling bad about something you did, or something you did not do, but you should have done. Dr. Brené Brown believes guilt is adaptive and helpful because it gets us to analyze something we've done or failed to do according to our values.[5] It makes us feel psychological discomfort that often leads to changed behavior.

Criminal lawyers may interact with people experiencing guilt and shame as they stand to be judged by the court and in some cases, literally labeled "guilty." The irony of guilt is that, like shame, one of the most therapeutic ways to deal with it is to tell your story to someone trustworthy. Yet, in the courtroom, we often keep the accused from testifying. Although we listen and understand as clients tell us their story, all the facts and details never get let out, often keeping the client trapped in guilt.

The restorative justice initiatives allowing victim and offender to participate in dialogue, help the clients heal from the guilt associated with their crimes. In our society we often send the guilty party away, locking them up, and metaphorically throwing them away. Thankfully these new initiatives are being used to help restore the humanity to those who have been the perpetrators and the victims of crime. Allowing both victim and offender to tell their stories can have great impact on the healing for everyone involved.

Lawyers and mediators have an ethical duty to keep confidences of their clients' past actions. As a mediator, I must sustain an extreme sense of confidentiality, as I must keep secrets if requested or required. However, keeping these daunting secrets to ourselves can sometimes bring us into a mild or moderate state of guilt or anxiety ourselves. If we have these feelings, and our clients do as well, we are suddenly swirling in that toxic, emotional environment. This environment is hard to escape as the confidences never escape.

Each lawyer needs a trusted confidante – a counselor, a clergyperson, or another lawyer, although that is controversial. We can't give all the details to these confidantes sometimes "changing the facts to protect the innocent," but we can give the big picture. If we as lawyers are not whole to begin with, treating our mind, body and spirit, these guilty secrets affect us. Each of us must find a safe outlet to release the negativity and guilt. My personal solution to this dilemma is to turn to prayer.

Apathy

Apathy is a state of indifference. It involves suppressing emotions and a lack of concern or interest, often resulting from a feeling of inadequacy. Apathetic clients may have a flat affect and may be reluctant to tell us their story.

Listening to apathetic clients is hard work. These clients may expect us to take charge as they choose to stay helpless. In addition to the listening, we must ask questions and pry answers. Although open-ended questions usually elicit the most information with lower calibrating clients, apathetic clients may benefit from more direct questions, similar to questions we use in depositions. However, all methods of questioning must be delivered softly, and in a non-confrontational or intimidating fashion.

Grief

Grief is the reaction to a severing of a love relationship. It may be by death, divorce, or other forms of loss. The love may be for a person, an object, a time of life, or some other aspect of one's experience. People in grief usually have a degree of sorrow that takes a toll on the mind, body, and spirit. The degree of grief is usually associated to the degree of attachment of the survivor to the person or object lost.

Grief is prevalent in our meetings with clients. We may be there with them to probate the will of a deceased loved one. We may mourn with them the disfigurement of his or her body in an accident. They may have lost the job they had for the better part of their life. They may have dissolved a marriage and lost time with their children. Grief, in some capacity or another, permeates the law office.

Again, one of the best curative measures for grief is to tell the story to someone trustworthy. I remember when my Dad died, my best friends in Arizona came to the house soon after. My very best friend there is a Jewish lawyer. She brought my other Jewish friends along and said, "We are here to make a shiva call." I had never heard of "shiva."

In the Jewish tradition, the family that has lost an immediate family member "sits shiva," meaning they stay in the house and mourn, while friends come to the house to sit and remember the deceased. Friends bring food and stay and visit with the family, all to provide comfort.

I will never forget the beauty of the support my Jewish friends gave me that day. I said, "I don't know how to 'sit shiva.'" My friend Laura said, "We just sit here with you and when you are ready to talk, we listen." For the next few hours my friends sat quietly while I spoke about my Dad, my grief, and my sorrow. They listened quietly and intently, saying very little. In fact, it was the most intensive listening I had ever experienced. As lawyers, we may take a lesson from this rich tradition.

In addition to the emotions just discussed, keep in mind that fear, desire, anger and pride have also been identified as lower calibrating emotions. As we look at these life draining emotions, it is interesting to notice that all of them begin to subside when people tell their story. Listening is most definitely one of the most important skills we can have as compassionate lawyers.

Where does empathy come into play?

The legal profession is changing. There are online forms, self-service centers, software such as Legal Zoom, and more people strive to save money, representing themselves pro se. People are looking for ways to avoid lawyers. If we keep doing business the way we have been, our profession will become disjointed in an ever-changing world.

According to lawyer and author Daniel Pink, in his book *"A Whole New Mind,"* "The attorneys who remain will be those who can tackle far more complex problems and those who can provide something that databases and software cannot – counseling, mediation, courtroom storytelling, and other services that depend on (right brain) thinking."[6]

What right brain skill do we need the most? Empathy.

It is perceived that lawyers are paid to be dispassionate representatives who only deal in facts. Pink worries that people in general may have been taught that empathy is a "softhearted nicety in a world that demanded hard-headed detatchment."[7] Lawyers have certainly been taught to have detatchment. We were never taught empathy in law school.

So, how do we operate in empathy? First, it is important to distinguish more fully the difference between sympathy – feeling bad for someone, and empathy – feeling bad with someone. Empathy requires an ability to appreciate another's suffering and sensing what it might be like to be that person. However, this can be difficult when we hear stories of someone bringing on the suffering themselves.
To overcome this barrier, it is helpful to approach the discussion by identifying what you have in common with the client. Although this may be difficult at first, if you put forth an effort, you can find something.

According to the Dalai Lama:

"Whenever I meet people I always approach them from the standpoint of the most basic things we have in common. We each have a physical structure, a mind, emotions. We are all born the same way, and we all die. All of us want happiness and do not want to suffer. Looking at others from this standpoint rather than emphasizing secondary differences such as the fact that I am Tibetan, or a different color, religion or cultural background, allows me to have a feeling that I'm meeting someone just the same as me. I find that relating to others on that level makes it easier to exchange and communicate with one another."[8]

Recently, I was appointed by the court to be a guardian ad litem in a custody dispute involving twin boys. The mother had vehemently resisted my appointment, although she did not know me. Her lawyer warned me that I would have an angry woman to deal with.

Although I usually meet both of the parents the first time, in this instance I thought it was important to meet first with the woman who was resisting my appointment. I called her and we had a friendly conversation, arranging to meet the following week.

When the mother showed up in my office, she shook my hand and entered my conference room. She was wearing a hijab head covering and burqa. I introduced myself, offered her some water and then we sat down to talk. "Before we begin, can you help me understand why you resisted my appointment as your guardian ad litem?"

"Because I have been discriminated against as a Muslim and because I dress like I do. People think that just because I am a Muslim I am a terrorist. I worry that because you have influence and some level of authority over my children, there could be danger if you are also prejudiced."

I listened intently to her and then grabbed the cross on my necklace. "See this?" I said. "I am a Christian and I know what you mean. Sometimes when people see it they believe that I am a radical conservative who imposes my views on everyone and tries to "save" them, whether they like it or not."

As we continued to discuss the situation, I told her I have raised three children. Before long, she relaxed. Our journey ahead would prove to be challenging, but I believe we each had a connection of mutual respect from that day forward.

Empathy grows

Empathy grows the more we get to know people. Clients often like to talk about their families and their lives. A client I worked with recently spent 10 minutes telling me the life story of her best friend. It had zero relevance to her legal matter. She summarized how much that friend meant to her throughout her life. I simply listened without interruption, thinking of my own friend Laura who was a strong beacon for me during my life's most turbulent times. Often times, we don't listen because stories and sidetracks take too long; however, they are the threads that build the connection of empathy. Sometimes you have to put yourself in "another's shoes" to understand. For some reason this client needed to tell me the friend's story before we could get to her own.

Another case involved a gorgeous nurse who struggled with addiction to pain pills, which she took from her clinic's samples. The pills became her evening "cocktail" to relax. Eventually she "shopped" for doctors to prescribe the pills. She had been in and out of rehab a few different times when I met her. As a person who hates to even take an aspirin, I could not imagine being in her condition. As she told me the story of her addiction I listened intently. Then, I thanked her for honoring me enough to share her story with me. "We are all fighting our demons," I told her. "Yours is prescription drugs, mine might be something else, another person's is something else still. I respect that you are fighting the good fight," I told her.

Can empathy be taught?

Medical school education is beginning to embrace the idea of physician empathy at the "story catching" phase of the patient's treatment. Dr. Rita Charon, a professor at Columbia University Medical School, launched the narrative medicine movement in 2001.[9] The program at Columbia requires that all second year medical students take a semester in narrative medicine where they learn to listen, empathically, to their patients' stories. Charon believes that doctors require narrative competence, which she describes as "the competence that human beings use to absorb, interpret, and respond to stories."[10]

Charon's students keep two charts on their patients – one is for the quantitative information and medical terminology and another as a narrative about the patient, as well as the medical student's own emotions.[11] The results show those who used the two chart method had better relationships with patients, better interviewing skills, and better technical skills than the students who did not use the dual charting method.[12]

Don't lawyers, as healers of human conflict, owe it to our "patients" to develop a similar "treatment plan?"

Touch

The other part of showing empathy is to actually touch your client. It may be as simple as shaking the client's hand when he or she enters your office. When was the last time someone shook your hand, and then placed the free hand on top of the handshake while looking you directly in the eye? This warm greeting can begin a connection with the client.

Although it is risky, we may further consider touching a client as he or she is telling a particularly sensitive part of their story. A touch of the forearm or the hand can demonstrate empathy, and strangely, it might freak out both the person administering the touch and the one receiving it. We live in a society where nobody touches anyone.

Women lawyers may have more societal license to use touch. By virtue of my age and gender, I feel I also have more license to pat a client on the back as they sob, or to give them a hug as they leave my office. I will never forget a client and his wife who asked if I would hold their hands and pray before they left our meeting. These efforts are not automatic, but a compassionate lawyer will be open to responding. Touch can be volatile of course, and discretion is critical.

Recently, the counties I practice in adopted electronic filing. Now, instead of all the lawyers meeting at the courthouse for pretrial Fridays, we operate from our remote offices, communicating via electronic filing and email. One of my former associates once commented about how happy I was after returning from the courthouse on pretrial Fridays, as I got to see my colleagues and chat with the judges and court attendants. Interacting with people by smiling, touching their arm, or shaking their hand all help us stay connected to each other.

Bringing Clarity to Chaos

Every person who comes to see a lawyer likely has some degree of fear. Chaos often erupts when people are fearful, as their minds are blurred and they have difficulty dissecting information. To tout legalese at a client during these times is inconsiderate and ineffective. Clients may not fully understand the information because their brains are "offline" because of the fear or stress.

The human brain is often called the "triune brain" because it is composed of three layers. It can be easily demonstrated by holding your hand in a fist facing yourself, thumb tucked in, wrist toward your body, four fingers wrapped closed down on top of thumb.

Now, look at the base of your wrist. We can call that the reptilian brain. It is the primate brain, which is responsible for breathing, digestion, posture, balance, "fight, flight, freeze" as well as other primitive responses. It houses the survival instinct.

Next, notice your thumb sitting across your palm, stretching to your pinkie finger. This represents the mamallian part of the brain, which is also called the limbic system. The limbic system is responsible for motivation and also feelings such as anger, fear, and emotions related to sexual behavior. This is the part of the brain that stores our emotional memories.

Finally, notice the closed four fingers closed down tightly over the thumb, enveloping the tight fist with the thumb stuck in the middle. The top fingers represent the neocortex brain or the "thinking brain." This part of the brain is responsible for language, reasoning, logic, and forward planning. The neocortex enables decision making and purposeful thinking.

When clients come to see us they are often "offline" from their neocortex. In your closed palm, now shoot your four top fingers skyward. The shooting fingers represent that the neocortex has gone offline, which happens as a result of fear and confusion. If that part of the brain is "offline," the client is left to make decisions with their lower functioning brain, which is either emotional or basic survival oriented. We cannot throw complex legal information at clients who are not thinking comprehensively. If we are not helping bring their neocortex back online, by speaking to them calmly and with compassion, they simply cannot process our information.

Some psychologists estimate that we operate in the neocortex, where we are clear minded, only 15% of the time.[13] That is, we are "offline" or engaged in lower functioning thinking 85% of the time. It is doubtful that our clients are operating in that 15% window when they are with us. Our job as compassionate lawyers is to assist clients to return to the "fingers down" stage and operate from their neocortex. One of the ways to do that is to take a complex subject matter and break it down slowly and carefully, using simple language.[5]

As a mediator I am often amazed how a lawyer will begin speaking legal shorthand with me, totally disregarding the client sitting at the table. I find that after that happens, I work much like a language interpreter. I turn to the client and say, "Jane what your lawyer is saying to me is..." Jane is looking at me like a deer in the headlights as I explain things to her. However, if I do this calmly, Jane starts to nod and understand. I always watch to see if the client needs further explanation, and may be discerning whether they are coming back online with their neocortex by gauging their response.

Help the client move from lower calibrating emotions to courage

In the work by Dr. Hawkins[6] the emotion that he found to be instrumental in moving from life draining to life enhancing was courage.[14] Courage seems to be the magic potion, and I have found that it is a game changer with my clients, just as it has been in my own life. Hawkins found that when people become courageous, they find the gateway from the lower level, life draining energies, to the higher level, life-sustaining energies.[15] Brené Brown's research also supports this.[16]

Courage

What is courage? The root of the word courage in Latin is cor, and in French it is Coeur, both words meaning "heart."[17] Its original definition was "to speak one's mind by telling one's heart."[18] Over time, it has changed to merge in our vocabulary with bravery, but it is actually quite different.[19]

Bravery is the ability to confront pain or danger without any feeling of fear. Soldiers going to the battlefield, or the citizens who ran into the twin towers on 9/11 demonstrate bravery. Courage, on the other hand, is a state of mind – it is a willful choice to face the problem head on, regardless of what happens. When one is courageous, he or she recognizes that the struggle to overcome the situation is worth it.

Author Brené Brown states, "Heroics is important and we certainly need heroes, but I think we've lost touch with the idea that speaking honestly and openly about who we are, and what we're feeling, and about our experiences (good and bad) is the definition of courage. Heroics is often about putting our life on the line. Ordinary courage is about putting our vulnerability on the line. In today's world that's pretty extraordinary."[20]

For Brown, courage means telling her story with all her heart.[21] As lawyers we can encourage our clients and those we work with to have courage. By creating a safe environment, listening with compassion and empathy, we help the client find his or her voice to become vulnerable.

One of the most powerful questions I ask a client or a party in mediation is "What is your greatest fear?" If I have built trust with the person and they see me as the compassionate lawyer, he or she will share their deepest fear 99% of the time. As we approach that fear with conversation and legal advice, they will often unearth other fears. The client often feels a relief, although the fear has not been alleviated. If I cannot alleviate the fear, I let them know that I will be facing it alongside them as their advocate; I am not emotionally entangled in their problem so that I will keep my clear-headed view at the forefront as we dive in with courage. I have witnessed actual physical changes in people when we get into the courage mentality. Their shoulders pin back and they sit up straighter.

I will never forget my very first jury trial as a young lawyer, where I was second chair with my Dad's law partner. It involved the death of a young man. We brought a negligence suit on behalf of his estate, and we had to work very closely with his mother. After a long arduous trial, the jury came back with a zero verdict. We had lost the trial. Of course I was devastated and my ego was in flux. More importantly, I was forlorn because his mother got no recovery. How would I face her?

A few weeks after the trial she showed up unannounced at the law office and the secretary buzzed me to tell me she was there. I sheepishly went into the lobby to see her. She handed me a pillow, embroidered meticulously with birds, and said, "I want you to have this. I will never forget how you described my Joey to the jury. You told them who he was and it was exactly him. I am grateful they got to know about my son." At that moment I understood that even when we lose cases, the impact we have on our client's worlds by virtue of the power we hold as lawyers cannot be underestimated. She had faced justice for her son with courage, and it helped her to begin her healing journey.

The easiest way to help a client reach courage, is to encourage them

Once courage is on board, higher emotions – neutrality, willingness, acceptance, and reason begin to appear. Neutrality, especially, creates substantial changes. Neutrality is when the client is open to new information and possibilities. As the advocate, I can then provide them with real solutions to their issues, and they listen. By simply giving them encouragement to persevere, they respond. Then, they plug in to the most important emotion: hope!

One of my clients became a troubled alcoholic during the time I represented her in her divorce. When the divorce was finalized she was seeking help, and living in sobriety. Years later she came back to me, in tears, because she had a relapse and her ex was fighting to reduce her parenting time. Although she was active in AA, I told her about Celebrate Recovery, a faith based program at a local church for people struggling with "hurts, hang-ups, and habits." She wanted to attend. I had never gone, but agreed to go with her.

When we went to the main meeting, we heard the message and the testimony of someone in recovery. Afterwards we broke up into separate meeting rooms by gender and then by "problem." I cannot begin to describe what I learned. I had a whole new perspective for people in recovery after hearing all the brave people at the meeting. I feel I gained a whole new perspective on those suffering with addictions and those with debilitating issues, such as depression and eating disorders.

My client was enthused about the program. Recently I saw her. She is still sober and just completed her PhD. My job as her lawyer was to provide her with resources, not to be her sponsor or accountability partner. I was to be her compassionate lawyer with boundaries.
Ironically, another client had similar issues. He confided that AA was not helping him as he had hoped. I mentioned Celebrate Recovery to him and told him if he wanted to go I would meet him there.

He emailed me two days before the meeting and said he would very much like to go. I emailed him back and left him a voicemail, providing him specifics on the time and location. On the day of the meeting, I waited in the church lobby for 30 minutes after our scheduled meeting time and he did not show up. Not only that, but he did not call me until our next client meeting, where he acted nonchalant and simply said "Sorry I was unable to go to the meeting."

I don't know how he is doing either, since his legal matter is long since closed, but I do know that I showed him compassion at a time he needed it. These stories demonstrate that our clients will do with our compassionate lawyering efforts what they choose. We simply dispense the medicine, but they must heal their own lives.

Establishing clear boundaries

As we move to compassion, we must be careful not to overshoot the boundary. In other words, although as lawyers we can be conduits of healing, we are not the people responsible for doing the healing. Our clients have to actively participate.

Trouble can happen when instead of being the guide to healing, we take it on for the client. In this day and age there are a lot of wounded people who are victims of emotional abuse and have not had primary nurturing. They may be looking to their lawyer to fill those needs for them.

How do we establish clear boundaries?

1. **Fire abusive clients**
   There are some clients who are abusive to their lawyer.
   I had a client who was so unhappy in her life, she was constantly sneering and pouting whenever we would meet.
   She was rude and abrupt and disparaging of me and my legal advice. I had no choice but to fire her.

   "I'm sorry but I don't think we are a good fit to be able to work together. I feel strongly that you are not confident in my ability to represent you and you deserve to have that security. I have tried to communicate effectively with you but I don't think I am very effective. You can find other lawyers who can help you on the state bar website but today I am terminating our attorney client relationship. I will refund your retainer, and will not charge you for today's meeting."

Sometimes it is too late in the game to terminate the client, because of court deadlines. But if it is not, you must take care of yourself. The work of a lawyer is too intense to take abuse. Many of us are afraid to fire clients for fear they will retaliate with an unfounded grievance with the bar association. However, to continue to represent such a person is self abuse.

2. **You are not there to fill your client's emotional needs**
   Being compassionate doesn't mean that you become the client's best friend. Some clients want you to be their family or to go out socially with them. Some may call and/or email incessantly. Others are looking to us to help meet many of their emotional needs.

Our job as lawyers is to dispense compassion during our professional interaction and not to rescue the clients from their sad lives. As we lead them to courage and higher calibrating emotions, we help them to face their problems honestly and in a goal oriented fashion. Those that are choosing to stay victims, and want us to support that, need to be managed firmly.

A good trigger as to whether you are a "resource" for the client or they are being overly needy is your level of resentment. Are you resentful that the client continues to call and push the boundary? Does the client fail to take "no" for an answer? Is the client acting like a victim, never able to take personal accountability or implement the recommendations you have made for them as you encourage them to take charge of their lives?

That being said, a few clients become friends after our professional relationship ends. These people are friends with clear emotional boundaries. Some send me annual Christmas cards or email me to say hello. Others are people I go out to dinner with on occasion to catch up. These relationships should be carefully chosen.

3. **Your "No" must be "No"**
   Once we open our hearts to clients, there is a danger that we will become attached to them. The best way to set boundaries is to say "NO." Sometimes when we are busy or stressed, or have demanding clients it is just easier to think we "should" say "yes." If we are not able to tell our clients clearly what we will and won't do, we are at risk of endangering our relationship and our health.

   The commitment for timely delivery of work product also deserves clear boundaries. If we promise a client a response we should do it in the agreed upon time, but it should not be a timeframe that we will be unable or stressed to meet. Clear expectations are essential when dealing with clients. And once we set the promised deadlines, we must adhere to them.

4. **Using our support staff to help us set boundaries**
   Having our staff help us set boundaries is a good idea, as long as we don't violate our boundaries with those staff people. It is never the responsibility of the support staff to explain our boundaries to the client. That is our job. Our staff can help us maintain the boundary and can also be a sounding board for us if we think a client is inappropriately pushing the boundary.

5. Boundaries take practice

I still remember one of my very first clients, who would not take no for an answer. We did not get the ruling he wanted on a motion, so he convinced me to do a motion to reconsider, against my better judgment. In the editing of it he persuaded me to be more biting than my instincts allowed. Every step of the way he was pushing the boundary for more intervention, overstepping prudent judgment and good legal practice. Yet I wanted to please my client and went along with everything.

All these years later I remember feeling used and abused by that client because of his own emotional neediness and anger. It took me years to learn to be direct with clients, in a loving way, and to set boundaries. If lawyers are unable to do that early on in their practice, they may not be able to learn the essence of healthy compassion.

Using our power wisely

Lawyers have real power. Compassionate lawyers have the power to change people's path and put them on a new life trajectory. This type of lawyering is also exhilarating to us. If we are to reclaim ourselves as conduits of healing, we need to embrace the unique influence we have on people in the time of crisis.

Chapter 7

Respect

Compassionate lawyers respect themselves, their families, their colleagues, the courts, and others

Among lawyers, the word "respect" stirs up questions about how to manage the delicate balance of treating others in a respectful manner without losing your "edge" in zealously representing clients. But isn't there a base level of respect all human beings desrve?

When a lawyer's ego gets the best of him or her, the essential "little people" seem to be forgotten. In moving toward compassion, we become more aware of all the people in our world and determine whether they are consistently receiving this base level of respect and dignity. As we evaluate respect within the legal profession, we begin at the top of the "authority totem pole."

The Court

Respect for the court means that lawyers are prepared, punctual, and professional. For many of our clients, the court is the last hope they have that someone (a judge or jury) will understand their story and dispense life-changing justice.

Lawyers need to be fully prepared to present their case to the court. Our clients don't often know whether the lawyer is prepared, or just how prepared he or she is. When we are in the courtroom, clients rely on us to know what we are doing. It seems that as long as the lawyer uses big words and looks confident, the client doesn't scrutinize the lawyer's level of preparation.

I have seen lawyers frantically slap on exhibit stickers five minutes before trial, as well as lawyers who don't know the case, but still parade in front of the judge and look like they are in charge. The lawyer must think if he or she just gets up, performs, and goes through the motions, the poor and clueless client won't know the difference because the client still "got a day in court."

In my own jurisdiction, temporary family law matters are handled in chambers and off the record. The lawyers sit across the desk from the judge and they each make their "pitch." I am shocked at the number of opposing lawyers that "shoot the breeze" with the judge as they hand out documents in a loose fashion and sit without any notes before them. This method of "lawyering" disrespects three important parties: the judge, by minimizing his or her authoritative presence; opposing counsel, who is there is to do important business; and oneself, as he or she looks sloppy.

The minute we enter those chambers or the courtroom, we are entering sacred ground. That is where justice is sought, and where our society believes that every American has an opportunity to be heard. Our clients entrust us to be there as their spokesperson, as freedom and personal liberties are at stake. The courtroom is not turf for lawyers to just "practice" because there are big dollars and big fees involved. The courtroom should be reserved for consummate professionals that come in reverence and preparedness, befitting of the highest caliber of our profession.

Lawyers need to be punctual. If we are prepared, including everything from regular sleep to avoiding procrastination, there should be no problem arriving to court on time. In addition, when the court adjourns for breaks, compassionate and respectful lawyers are punctual in returning to the courtroom. This includes our clients as well, as they should be well informed of the court process and what to expect.

I once went to a pretrial conference on a pro bono case I had been assigned through the volunteer lawyers program, and the other side was pro se (appearing without a lawyer). I was running late from my office and made it to the courtroom 10 - 15 minutes late. I apologized profusely to the court and was glad to see the pro se had not shown up. I thought the judge would overlook my tardiness and maybe even commend me for doing a Volunteer Lawyers Program (VLP) case. Instead, he fined me $50 for being disrespectful to the court. I remember complaining, but ultimately I realized the judge was right. Who was I to disrespect the judge's time? And who was I to disrespect my pro bono client, minimizing his case because it was a "freebie?"

Lawyers should look and act like a professional, honoring courtroom protocol. Before electronic filing, a particular judge in my jurisdiction required men to wear a necktie to get an order signed, even if no hearing was involved. In fact, he was known to send men away if they weren't wearing a tie. As a woman, I always wore a skirt or dress when I needed to do anything at the courthouse in front of that judge, unless it was an impromptu trip. Now, I have developed the habit to always wear a skirt or dress when I am scheduled to be in court.

These instances made me realize how sloppy we, as lawyers, have become in the way we hold ourselves out to the public. My Dad always wore a full suit and tie to the office. He looked like a lawyer should look. I think we all act differently depending on how we are dressed.

Compassionate lawyers are also cognizant of their professionalism outside of the courtroom. I have seen lawyers come to my office dressed in jeans for mediation. Perhaps one of the most unprofessional sights I have seen was when a lawyer came to mediation underdressed and late, carrying a burger, fries, and super sized soda pop. He ate lunch while telling me about the client's case. Sadly, the client didn't even seem to care or notice. Shouldn't clients be entitled to more than this?

Judges are lawyers, too

Respect in the courtroom works both ways, as judges are lawyers, too. Judges who run a tight courtroom are well respected. On the other hand, when judges show up late, everyone is forced to wait, causing anxiety and nervousness to build up. This has a significant effect on our clients.

127

Personally, my favorite judges are those who are punctual and well prepared by studying the case file thoroughly before the trial or hearing, and who listen intently during the argument. On the other hand, when a judge dozes on the bench or seems to be on their computer throughout the trial, I am unsure how to explain and assure my client that he or she got a "fair trial." Calibrating high should be a given for our judges. Our system is banking on their wisdom, intelligence, and most of all, their compassion to administer justice.

Court clerks and staff

Those of us who interface with the court also know that there are numerous court personnel who cross our paths – from the clerk behind the filing desk, to the judge's bailiff or court attendant, to the court reporter. The staff is instrumental in guiding us through the court system.

My Dad told me from my first day as a lawyer to learn the names of the courthouse staff. I always watched him inquire about their lives and families when I went there with him. When my Dad was close to death, my family got a call from the clerk's office inquiring, on behalf of a group of them, how he was doing. Later a few ladies from the clerk's office told me Dad called them early on in his illness to inform them he would not be at the courthouse anymore and to thank them for the fine level of service they rendered in all of his years working with them.

A lawyer friend of mine recently told me he learned a lot about practicing law from "the two Betty's." Two court clerks named Betty led him through the administrative protocol at the courthouse when he was a young lawyer. Even with the advent of electronic filing, I still have my go-to clerks who help me figure out the nuances of the system. They have even rescued me from foolish mistakes on occasion.

Support staff

Most lawyers have an assistant, a secretary, and/or a paralegal. Some lawyers have multiples of each position within their support staff. I know lawyers who would be substantially less effective without their assistants. In fact, with permission of the lawyer, sometimes I call his or her competent assistant to ask questions.

When my county converted to e-filing, there were two wonderful women who were legal assistants for other lawyers, but helped me with my ridiculous questions. Ironically, they are "the two Joni's." They willingly and kindly explained certain procedures and supplied me with specialized forms. In response to their efforts, I gave each of them a small gift to express my thanks.

Recently, after settling a case with opposing counsel, I suggested his strong assistant prepare the first draft of the Qualified Domestic Relations Order (QDRO) on our case. He declined, letting me know she was struggling through a difficult time and was feeling overwhelmed.

I took the opportunity to email her, letting her know that the document she had prepared in advance of the negotiation of our case was instrumental in a smooth settlement, and thanking her for her fine quality of work. I did not tell her that the lawyer had told me about her struggles, but just wanted to give her a boost at a time when she was low. My extra effort took one minute. The secretary emailed back how appreciative she was of my email.

I believe lawyers often overlook their own support staff. A moment of being friendly, expressing thanks, or inquiring about their wellbeing really costs nothing but makes a huge difference in their lives.

Many lawyers work long hours and may struggle with a healthy lifestyle, but it is important that we do not expect our staff to do the same. Expecting staff members to respond to calls, texts, or emails at wee hours of the morning or night, or to work on weekends and evenings consistently, is disrespectful.

Lawyers respecting other lawyers

Disrespect among our colleagues may show up in overly aggressive approaches, but there are also subtleties.

1. **Respect for lawyers that are on a different level**

   Many judges are my age. In fact, some in my jurisdiction were my law school classmates. After practicing for so many years, they know me by first name. I have an outgoing personality, as I usually talk and joke with everyone, including the judges. However, I realize there is a time and place for this. Young and new lawyers, or even lawyers from other counties, don't usually have a close relationship with the judges, and may feel awkward laughing and joking with a judge. Therefore, if an opposing lawyer expresses familiarity with the judge, it may be perceived that the lawyer and the judge are "friends." As a result, we must try to be aware of when these situations happen and tone it down so as to be mindful not to embarrass the other lawyer.

   Conversely, younger lawyers may not realize the uneasiness some lawyers have around innovation in the practice, such as use of technology and social media. While younger lawyers are comfortable with electronic filing, older lawyers may rely on secretaries and law clerks to understand those processes. When young lawyers are talking about those issues, they may be unaware additional explanation may be necessary. Many older lawyers feel uncomfortable raising their lack of knowledge on some things that the younger lawyer takes for granted.

2. **Respect when working on a matter**

   Outside of the judge's eye, lawyers may ask for a professional courtesy. In my jurisdiction, the order for pretrial conference requires specific documents to be exchanged prior to the pretrial conference. One lawyer told me that as pretrial approached, he called opposing counsel, leaving a friendly reminder of the approaching deadline. However, the opposing counsel failed to respond to subsequent calls and emails, until just before the pretrial when they sent formal discovery to get what was already court ordered to be produced under the pretrial order. In these situations, compassionate lawyers will recognize opportunities when they can accommodate opposing counsel.

The age-old complaint of lawyers not returning phone calls doesn't apply just to the clients. There are lawyers in my community who are notorious for not returning opposing counsel's calls, not responding to letters, and taking long periods of time to move the case forward. Then, when they do decide they want to move the case, they surface again as though nothing has happened.

In addition to being disrespectful toward the other lawyer, it is a disrespect to both of the clients. It is very hard to explain to your client why his or her case is not moving. A compassionate lawyer doesn't want to throw their colleague under the bus as being the cause of the case stalling out, but you also can't cover for the other lawyer. The failure to respond may be a strategic move to delay or cause frustration or impatience, but a returned phone call with a simple message that the lawyer is not in a position to move the case forward preserves respect between the lawyers.

3. **Issues between lawyers**

I have chosen only one lawyer friend to vent to about other lawyers claiming "vault." Beyond that, when other lawyers talk about each other in front of us, compassionate lawyers don't get into the fray.

By the same token, if we are face-to-face with a lawyer and gossip erupts, we should not be afraid to speak up and avoid the situation. To simply respond, "My experience has not been the same," is a subtle way to let a lawyer know you don't want to gossip. We have all learned that if you can't say something nice, don't say anything at all. Lawyers are above such lower level energy.

131

Respect may also include taking action when another lawyer's actions may be inappropriate or potentially harmful for him or herself. For example, one of my closest lawyer friends began to drink heavily early in his practice. He was letting matters slip and had a grievance pending against him. I grew worrisome as it continued, so I called his wife to tell her I considered reporting him to the lawyer's assistance program to get confidential help for his drinking. She panicked and thought it was a horrible idea, concerned that the program would damage his practice more than it would help him. She asked me to not take any action.

I regrettably didn't pull the lawyer aside to tell him I was worried about him and his alcohol use, as I feared to get involved. I also never called the lawyers assistance program. Now, that particular lawyer has lost his license to practice law. I often wonder if we, a group of his concerned lawyer friends, had confronted him, spoken with him directly, and encouraged him to heal his life, whether he would have had a different life story. Instead of coming together to help our fallen colleague, as a compassionate group of friends, lawyers in the community ridicule our fallen colleagues, and the comments I hear are not compassionate. It seems that to boost their own egos, lawyers, in general, feed off the failure of another.

Approaching a lawyer in truth is not easy. There are lawyers in most communities who everyone knows are untruthful and questionably unethical. If you asked a group of 20 lawyers in your area to name the most under-handed and difficult to deal with lawyer in town, you would have the same person's name mentioned 99% of the time. Personally, I would want to know people thought of me that way. However, rarely does one confront the lawyer directly. If you mention to a colleague the possibility of going to this lawyer, in truth and love, to encourage a change in attitude and to let the lawyer know (s)he has a poor reputation in the community, nobody will volunteer to do it. Although it may be difficult and awkward to approach someone, it is a compassionate and thoughtful thing to do.

4. **Respect for lawyer's families**
We can also respect our colleagues by honoring their families. When my Dad passed away and other lawyers attended the funeral, I felt warmth and comfort as they spoke kind words of him. To this day, I cherish a hand-penned, thoughtful note from a lawyer I did not know, telling me what a fine lawyer my Dad was. He said how much he respected my father, and how his clients respected him. It spoke to me in a way all the other sympathy cards did not.

Now, I make it a point to tell a bereaved family that I am a lawyer and what kind of a lawyer their deceased loved one was and what a difference he or she made. If I don't know the family well, I always let them know that as a fellow lawyer, I realize the sacrifices they made due to the demands of the job, as well as all the grateful clients that appreciate their sacrifices.

Respecting our clients and others

We have already discussed that in respecting our clients we must listen, pay attention, and care for them. But, more can always be done.

1. **Following the client's objectives -- let them be involved**
Some lawyers believe every case is the lawyer's case and the client should just "follow the leader." One lawyer I interviewed said he occasionally yells at his client when the client won't listen. He believes the client is paying for his legal judgment and once the game plan is designed, the client must comply.

Compassionate lawyers can be role models for healthy problem solving by respecting each other, trusting each other and using methods to resolve disputes that may be nontraditional. Litigation is our trusty fallback and I often tell clients the only ones who enjoy trial and get their jollies there are the lawyers. In the courtroom we are strong warriors, involved in skill and endurance, and we are performing to an audience. All of those factors get our egos pumped, and our finest skills front and center. Unfortunately our clients all hate trial. They are fearful there, it costs them a lot of money and they feel totally out of control. Since we like it there, we tend to lead them there because it's our familiar venue.

However, compassionate lawyers are team players with clients. Just like a coach, the lawyer may need to discuss the client's impact on the case for failure to follow the game plan. Reality is that the case can be fluid and the client's objectives can be as well. As the client gets into the lawsuit or legal negotiation, needs may change as the result of unfolding information. We need to be vigilant about hearing what the client needs, ensuring he or she is emotionally fortified and practical, as well as observing the changes ourselves, and then talking these issues out with the client.

In the past several years, mediation has popped up as a first resort to dispute resolution. I first began working in the field of mediation and alternative dispute resolution in 1987. When I found out about the process, and became trained in it, I was exhilarated that it gave me an opportunity to help clients resolve disputes in what seemed like a healthier, more empowering manner. It allowed the clients to be intricately involved in their own destiny. Putting the mediator in the middle of the dispute gave the parties a buffer for the emotional effect of word exchange and provided a much needed "clear head" in the room to direct the conversation.

Early on, many lawyers were resistant to the idea that
the dance was being changed. Instead of being rewarded
for their ability to do battle, they would be valued for their
peacemaking abilities. The problem was that most of them
had not been trained in peacemaking, and had no earthly
idea how to do it. Further, there was restlessness in
knowing how the field would unfold. Would clients go to
mediation by themselves and displace lawyers in their
role? Would suggesting mediation make a lawyer look
weak or ill-prepared to go to trial? Over time compassionate lawyers have come to realize the value of the mediation
process to clients.

2. **Talking about others**
It is not surprising that lawyers talk amongst themselves
about clients. I recently had to break up a gossip fest in my
office between two lawyers who played client geography to
determine they had mutual clients in a juicy marital affair.
In other words, one represented the paramour of the
other's client in the paramour's divorce. They both went
on to disparage their clients, judging them as "bat s**t
crazy" and giggling about the extent of dysfunction.
I squeamishly interrupted and suggested we move on
to the business at hand.

I get nervous as lawyers become entangled with client
gossip at mediations. While clients sit in their respective
rooms, lawyers may call a "meeting" in a third room, but
end up chatting and catching up. Compassionate lawyers
save these collegial conversations for after the hearing,
mediation, or other event involving the clients.

3. **Keeping it private**
There is also a challenge for those of us who run into
clients, or others we have talked to in our legal capacity
in public. The truest form of confidentiality is that nobody
should even know who our clients are. They should also

never know that someone came to see us in our legal capacity as a lawyer, even if they are not retained as a client. My mother used to get frustrated, as she would refer someone to my Dad then later ask if he was representing him or her. He could never tell her. In my own experience, I remember a former client approached me at the mall and gave me a hug. My ex-husband was with me at the time and asked how we knew each other. The client and I quietly and awkwardly looked at each other, as I responded with a vague, "You know what a small community we live in!" then quickly changed the subject.

4. Legalese

If lawyers asked their clients what it is that they fear most, it is probably something along the lines of "I have no clue what anything means, so I rely on you." Therefore, compassionate lawyers must be sensitive to the wording in the documents we provide for clients. "Legalese" is easy to slip into our consultations, letters, and documents if we are not careful. We know the subtle differences between such words as "shall," "will," and "may," but our clients have no idea. We must remember that our clients will refer to the legal documents that we drafted, even after our representation. Chances are they refer to them when possible conflict arises. We need to write in simple terms.

One of the reasons legalease often gets the better of lawyers is that we rely heavily on forms. However, using forms over and over can cause us to rely on them without adapting them to the client's case. I am reminded of a contract I recently drafted for a coach in helping me stay on schedule to write this book. Since I was the lawyer, he asked me to propose the contract we would use. I developed a contract and met with him to go over it. I thought I'd streamlined the form contract I used, but at the end of my reading through it with him he forthrightly

told me that it was very complicated. And he was right.
I could have made it much easier if I had drafted it from
scratch using a solid form to cross check its content.
I had taken the lazy route.

Our families

Compassionate lawyers are considerate of their families. Most of us
make a comfortable living and our families live comfortably. But as
they say, money does not buy happiness – our respect must extend
further when it comes to those closest to us.

Workaholism is a struggle for many lawyers. Setting boundaries that
are respectful to our families is essential. I remember my Dad being
home for dinner 90% of the time when I was growing up. I also know
there were times he had to go back to the office after he put us to bed,
or when he was awakened in the middle of the night to bail a client out
of jail. He never missed an important family event, dance recital, or
school concert.

One of my colleagues once told me he was out of town for a three-
week trial. His wife reported to him that one night at the dinner table,
their young son looked toward the empty chair and asked, "Whatever
happened to Dad anyway?" Ironically, the lawyer died in his 50's.

With the advent of technology, we constantly check our smartphones
and refuse to disconnect, even after office hours and during family
time. Some lawyers even give clients personal cell phone numbers.
However, it is essential we set boundaries and pay respect that is due
to our supporting families. Rest, relaxation and fun with them is one of
life's greatest gifts that should not be missed.

The other thing that cannot be over-emphasized is that our families
affect us. When our loved ones struggle with substance abuse, depression, or poor sleep habits, those things impact us. We are impacted
with their lower calibrating energy and the gyrations we make to help
take care of them. As many baby boomer lawyers find themselves in

"the sandwich generation," we are taking care of kids, parents, spouses or partners, and all our wounded clients, too. They look to us for our strength and problem solving abilities.

Compassionate lawyers are juggling a lot of responsibilities. Failure to give focus to those things that drain our energy, even unknowingly, is part of what causes us to burnout, blowout, or look for unhealthy ways of coping with our stress. Be awake. Be aware. Respect yourself enough to make self-care a priority in mind, body and spirit.

Boundaries revisited

With regard to respect, lawyers must set boundaries to ensure that our efforts toward respecting one another are not abused. I am often reminded of a line from my favorite prayer: teach me to act firmly and wisely, without embittering or embarrassing others. That action implies a firm representation, but it does not mean we let people "run us over."

Setting clear boundaries is essential in all aspects of our compassionate walk. Just because we are compassionate does not mean we have the energy or ability to cope with another's disrespect. If "compassion begins at home" then we must guard our mind, body, and spirit, as well as our inherent values and integrity. There is a difference between being compassionate and being nice. Being nice is a courtesy – it is a way of interacting with people. Being compassionate is to feel some-one's pain and try to alleviate his or her suffering. However, the danger is in going deeper and making your own happiness and quality of life depend on how the person is doing.

None of these respect considerations are earth shattering new concepts, but these are the actions that are dispensed by influential compassionate lawyers. Making the small changes is the first step in reviving the dignity of our wounded profession.

Empowering

**Compassionate lawyers live and lead well,
empowering experienced lawyers and mentoring
the younger generation of lawyers**

When my Dad was diagnosed with idiopathic pulmonary fibrosis, I moved my parents into my home and worked with Hospice during the seven months I cared for him. Since he was bedridden, I joked that I could hold him captive for the long awaited father/daughter talks. One of the first things I asked him was whether he was glad he was a lawyer. He paused only briefly and replied, "Yes. I loved being a lawyer." He went on to describe positive ways that he impacted people's lives in his work as a lawyer.

As individual lawyers, we must ask ourselves, at the end of our lawyer lives would we also answer, "Yes. I loved being a lawyer?" More importantly, we must ask ourselves as we approach the ends of our practices, "Will I finish well"?

Finishing well

Finishing well is to fulfill our individual "calling" in the law and leave a legacy for the legal profession to come. As a lawyer, I never set my sights on the end of my career. Instead I focused on the exact moment in time to stay afloat in the competitive and stressful environment. Paul Leavenworth, the man who coached me throughout the writing of "*The Compassionate Lawyer*," introduced me to the concept of finishing well. In fact, many concepts in this chapter are his concepts, which I have taken and related to lawyers.

While I was in a workshop of Paul's, I realized we don't dream of our own legacy. We don't envision or dream of what we will leave for future generations of lawyers. Again, this is due to the lifestyle of the profession, as some of us literally work until we drop. When I was an associate at my first law firm job, one of the senior partners had literally dropped dead at his desk.

Each of us must also ask ourselves, "At the end of my career, what will I have contributed to the legal profession?"

It is disappointing to find that studies show only one in four leaders finish well.[1] We can all name lawyers who have "finished well," others who have "finished so-so," as well as others who have finished poorly. Even when there have been some missteps along the way, we can still finish well. Former President Bill Clinton is a good lawyer case study. How would you rate his finish?

To finish well, we must recognize derailing events that may erupt during our career, and then identify ways to eliminate the effects.

Blowout

Many lawyers start strong, but may lose steam toward the end of their career. They may become victims of blowout, a phenomenon of losing touch with our own integrity. This is common among lawyers because we are constantly testing our integrity as we persuasively argue and advocate for our client's cause. Under such circumstances, we find it acceptable to wade into the grey areas.

Some lawyers may become selfish or greedy, or feel a sense of inadequacy. Some may realize they are not "all that" as a lawyer and settle with a meager career. Conversely, other lawyers may realize that selfish ambition is derailing. Striving to make partner, shareholder, or gain other recognition provides us with reasons to compromise, and become selfish or greedy.

A life of incongruity may cause us to feel hypocritical. We may repetitively tell our children not to do drugs, yet have no hesitation to suppress evidence on behalf of a drug dealer client. We may teach Sunday school, yet convince ourselves that spinning facts in a particular manner is not lying. Living this way can stir an inner angst that eats away over time. Although we may recognize many of these cracks in our own integrity, we rationalize, "I am still supporting the Constitution!"

Burnout

Burnout is similar to blowout, but commonly occurs during mid-career. This phenomenon occurs when burdens take a toll on our professional and personal lives. The first symptom of burnout is that mind, body, and spirit care begins to erode. We overwork and take on too much, failing to eat, sleep, or exercise, and we become disconnected from our spirit. In turn, we become discouraged or depressed.

As work becomes a daily dread, a lawyer may begin to wonder if there is a better life outside the practice of law. However, the lawyer may feel stuck, refusing to end up as the "former lawyer."

If one does not listen to his or her inner voice, the lawyer becomes easily irritated with others and ends up isolated from the world. The lawyer may become unhappy with his or her work and slip into engaging in unethical or questionable practices.

Plateauing

In mid to late career, lawyers may lose zest for the practice. They lose nerve and play it safe, billing hours and collecting a paycheck, so as not to ruin a good thing. While this may have been idealistic in the past, it is now status quo. This phenomenon is called plateauing.

When one fails to continue practicing in vibrant and fruitful ways, it often stems from uncertainty. Perhaps prior failures have made it too dangerous to take risks. Further, many of us do not trust that lawyers can change and evolve within our personal lives and in our practices.

One's plateau may also stem from arrogance. Organizational researcher Jim Collins in *"How the Mighty Fall,"* identifies that "plateauing and decline actually occur when people become arrogant, regarding success virtually as an entitlement, and they lose sight of the true underlying factors that created success in the first place."[2]

Personally, I believe plateauing is most dangerous for the legal profession. We cannot be set on autopilot to live a life of safety and mediocrity, especially when our profession calls for change. We can't thwart innovation or new ways to problem solve, which may be hidden or shut down in cubicles or overworking firms. Instead, we must be respectful of innovation within our profession.

At the end of this chapter I have included a self-test to determine whether you may be suffering from blowout, burnout, or plateauing.

Be alert to the "derailers"

What is it that may cause lawyers to not finish well? Studies show that "poor finishers" dealt with the following impediments:

- Sexual immorality

- Misuse of finances

- Abuse of power

- Self-centered pride

- Problems with marriage and family

- Life and work plateauing

- Emotional wounding

In order to avoid these de-railing events and help others do the same, we must constantly be checking ourselves and our behavior.

Compassionate lawyers are accountable to our profession and to one or more accountability partners

The most valuable concept I have employed in my quest to finish well has been to connect with an accountability partner. When I looked at my life from the outside in, I knew I did not have enough people to keep me on task and challenge me to review various areas of my life.

One of my accountability partners has been my priest. For over 20 years I have met with Father Andrew to assess my life as well as the cracks in my foundation that, at times, threatened to ruin my life, both as a person and as a lawyer. As our relationship progressed, I felt accountable to myself and to someone who could track my progress. Father Andrew was the first person to tell me I needed to write this book.

More recently, I gained a second accountability partner; the man who also encouraged me to write this book and coached me along the way. In our monthly meetings and weekly emails, I know that someone is monitoring my work and holding me to a high standard. Without his support I may not have had the courage or persistence to write this book, or to fight off my own plateauing.

Most importantly, as lawyers, we must hold ourselves accountable to our profession. A lawyer's failure to speak out for higher standards and compassionate lawyering is intolerable if we wish to impact the world in the way we are uniquely situated to accomplish. The failure to hold ourselves individually and collectively accountable leads to fewer of us finishing well.

Compassionate lawyers help the younger lawyers "start well"

We need to help younger or less experienced lawyers "start well." I wonder what my career would be like if someone had sat down with me at the beginning of my law practice and simply asked questions such as, What do you want the end of your career to look like? What do you worry might get in the way of that picture? How will you avoid burnout, blowout or plateauing? What can I do to help you maintain accountability? Or, most importantly, what might my life be like if someone had told me that people can live a strong life, but miss their destiny?

I have several law students and young lawyers I mentor and/or coach. I discuss all of these things with my mentees. I also share where I have gone wrong and try to give them connections to other lawyers and community resources. I listen to them and repeat back to them what I hear them saying, often adding whatever widom I can offer. One of my law student mentees intently told me that nobody in her life had ever sat and just listened to her.

In the book *"Connecting,"* Paul Stanley and Robert Clinton give Ten Commandments of Mentoring: [3]

1. **Establish the mentoring relationship**
   In deciding whom to mentor, people with similar skill sets or natural abilities tend to be attracted to each other. The way I picked two of the students I am currently mentoring is that each of them made a courageous statement in class, at the risk of being seen as "different" by their peers.

2. **Jointly agreeing on the purpose and expectations**
   In order to avoid conflict or hard feelings, the mentor and mentee must have a clear understanding of the scope and purpose of their relationship. For example, will this be an open-ended, ongoing relationship, or is it for a limited period of time? Will it be on an as-needed basis, or will specific meetings be scheduled? It is essential the expectation be clarified so the relationship has a purpose.

   For some young lawyers I am the equivalent of "phone a friend." In a formal mentoring relationship with a student, I am working through a workbook on a life skill. I am also helping another student work through mind, body, and spirit issues, as well as identifying his particular "calling" in the law. As an adjunct professor of law, I always offer to my students to serve as a lifetime resource once they begin to practice. Students who took my class more than five years ago still call to discuss ideas and cases. Recently I got a call from a baby lawyer who was about to have her first full evidentiary hearing. She was petrified and felt insecure approaching any lawyers in her firm to discuss her fears and insecurities. I coached her and encouraged her, texting her the morning of the hearing to get her psyched up. We debriefed afterwards and she was exhilarated, but also very intuitive about how to improve.

3. **Maintain the relationship with regularity**
   Identify regularity of meetings, and address the types of interaction and boundaries of contact. I have found monthly meetings and weekly accountability emails on Fridays to work well.

4. **Accountability**
   What are the parameters of accountability? What if meetings are cancelled? What if "homework" that is assigned is not completed before the meeting? What if there is only a "half baked" effort?

   To enhance accountability, make your expectations clear, be sure the mentee has heard them, be consistent in enforcing expectations, recognize that sometimes circumstances erupt, and make adjustments if there are consistent problems.

5. **Communication**
   Healthy communication comes in the form of encouragement, honesty, letting the young lawyer know you believe in him or her, and taking pride in accomplishments. If tough conversations must take place, they should be made in love and compassion.

6. **Confidentiality**

   Clarify confidentiality. As lawyers we are used to this, but what if we find our mentee needs to have an intervention or needs help through the lawyers assistance program? What if they have delved into their trust account? Create a clear understanding of expectations.

7. **Life cycle**

   Define the length of the mentoring relationship. It is also good to communicate regularly about how the relationship is going.

8. **Evaluation**

   Periodically evaluate the relationship and clarify expectations because perceptions and/or circumstances can change.

9. **Modification**

   Don't be afraid to modify expectations. You may need to slow down or refocus expectations because of things happening in and/or outside of the mentoring relationship.

10. **Closure**

    Bring a timely closure to the formal mentoring relationship. At the end of the mentoring relationship, clarify closure and relational issues. Will you stay friends? Will you be available if there is a "flare up" in the mentee's life? This conversation may be uneasy, but feelings can get hurt if relational terms are not clarified.

What I have come to realize is that if each of us invests in only two students or young lawyers, and in the future each of them invest in two, the possible impact of an infrastructure of coaching and mentoring law students and young lawyers will have an incredible impact on the quality of the profession. Even if each compassionate lawyer coached or mentored only one lawyer or law student, the exponential reach of compassionate lawyers could literally change the world.

I have been involved in some underwhelming attempts at formal law school or bar association mentoring programs. I get assigned a mentee, we meet at a "pep rally" and then I may see him/her one other time before we are disconnected and the mentoring ends.

Mentoring is meant to be a more formal process where the relationship is transformational, and all participants come to a healthier understanding and experience of their potential as individuals and lawyers, members of their social networks and members of a community who serve and empower others.

You may have already concluded you don't have time for this, but before abandoning the idea, keep in mind that there are different kinds of mentoring: formal mentoring, where regular meeting and communication takes place, or occasional/passive and distant mentoring, where communication may be via email or Skype only.

The content of the mentoring relationship involves some basic levels of support including:

1. Encouragement

2. Sounding board

3. Evaluation

4. Perspective

5. Advice

6. Networking connections

7. Guidance

8. Healing

Mentoring at different levels

Law clerks

Most law clerks, when they enter their clerkship, have never set foot in a corporate law department, law firm, or legal office. Therefore, they are anxious to soak in everything they see from those who are in power.

Whether it is intentional or not, clerks that work in firms or companies will take on the practice skills of the seasoned lawyers influencing them. Even though this is not a formal mentoring relationship, it is mentoring through imitation. Many skills are not learned in law school, but are on the job skills. Seasoned lawyers that show law clerks "how it is done" may be the only model clerks have to practical aspects of the practice. Sadly, many law clerks are stuck in the back room with no training or mentoring.

Rather than "best practices" which are sometimes studied in business models, many lawyers learn at the foot of the lawyer they work for. As the lowest person on the totem pole in the law firm structure, the law clerk is beholden to practice in the ways the other lawyers have chosen. If those lawyers have taken on unhealthy lifestyles and expect the same of law clerks, the impact on lawyers' lives can put them on a trajectory of unhealthy habits.

A compassionate lawyer realizes that everything they model and teach, from billing to client interaction to healthy habits, is a blueprint for a young lawyer's professional life.

Baby lawyers

When I have a trial and the opposing counsel is a young lawyer, I do my best to provide feedback. This is more "informal mentoring." My Dad taught me as a young lawyer that after the case, when the decision is inked, to solicit critique from the judge. Although we may not realize it, this interaction is also informal mentoring.

On the other hand, there are lawyers who show young lawyers how not to practice. In a trial of mine, the opposing lawyer sent his associate to do the dirty work at negotiations on the day of the trial. The senior lawyer was uncooperative, as he failed to return my calls and was rather unprofessional. The associate lawyer and I settled the case and went into the courtroom to dictate the settlement on record.

As we left the courtroom, I called the young lawyer over away from the clients. I told him, "Don't ever practice law like the lawyer that put you up to this. You are better than that. Always play with high integrity." I told him specifically what was unacceptable about that lawyer's practice style. I don't know if he took the advice or not, but I felt he deserved to have someone point out there is another way of doing business. In that moment, I felt that I owed the young lawyer informal mentoring.

Lawyers

Although I can hardly be called a young lawyer, I also have a mentor in the practice. This lawyer is the one and only person I can talk to about other lawyers and my frustrations with them, in a confidential manner. I chose this mentor because he is compassionate. A compassionate mentor who hears a lawyer suffering with regard to other lawyers does two important things: he or she validates your feelings and then helps you realize the other lawyer's suffering in a way that encourages compassion for both of you.

My mentor is also a resource for me to discuss whether I am handling a case properly. If I get that inner voice that tells me maybe I am getting perilously close to an ethical boundary, he will listen and advise. I value my mentor's integrity, so I trust his judgment.

Compassionate lawyers see that without mentoring, young lawyers may not start well

Right now in the legal industry, jobs are tight. Furthermore, new lawyers may have upwards of $150,000 in student loan debt. In turn, those that cannot find a firm job may go hang a shingle and take any clients they can get. Without a mentor or "go to" lawyer, they may flounder.

Some lawyers hang their head in disgust, frightened with how ill-equipped these lawyers are to be on their own. However, few of them step forward to guide, mentor, or assist these young lawyers. Compassionate lawyers recognize that we must step forward and that we have a vested interest in helping these young lawyers start well.

In writing this book, I spoke at length with one of the most feared, aggressive attorneys in my community. I asked him to tell me about his mentor(s) within his legal practice. He replied that he had no mentors. In essence, he taught himself to practice law. Without anyone modeling the practice for him, he became the antithesis of a compassionate lawyer. Would it have been different if someone had taken this lawyer under his or her wing? As compassionate lawyers, we must reach out to lawyers, younger or older that need guidance.

If assisting young lawyers has a positive impact, we need to be aware that disparaging these lawyers can also have a devastating, negative impact on the trajectory of a young lawyer's practice. A lawyer friend of mine with 40 years experience, hearkened back to his first lawyer job as a legal aid attorney. For his very first trial, he was thrown into the case at the eleventh hour and had to hustle to get prepared. When trial came, my friend set up shop at the counsel table. His opposing counsel, a seasoned veteran, took his place at the other counsel table. My friend went over and extended his hand, having never personally met the other counsel.

Opposing counsel refused to extend his hand in return, but looked my friend square in the eyes and said "F-You!" Needless to say, my friend was shocked. One might argue it was a masterful job of psyching out the other lawyer just before trial. Another might argue that his opponent acted inappropriately.

Young lawyers getting out of law school are looking for their game legs. Some young lawyers aspire to make their mark and as a result they often come out of the gate overly aggressively. It is almost as if they believe a true lawyer has to be a bulldog. This is a prime example of a misunderstanding of what it means to be a lawyer. I suspect many of these lawyers are uncomfortable in this role, but they are operating in their deferential style, as they think it is expected of them. Judges in my jurisdiction have made comments that they are troubled by this approach by young lawyers.

Another young lawyer I know is an associate at a big law firm in town. At the onset of a recent deposition, opposing counsel, a lawyer from a firm where the young lawyer clerked during law school, said "I know you clerked at our firm when you were a law student. I also know you weren't offered a position with our firm. Glad to see you were able to find a job." When I heard this story I was instantly disappointed. Such a comment is completely degrading and unnecessary.

Young lawyers likely feel insecure and unsure as most firms put their baby lawyers in an office and challenge them to bill. Then bill some more. They may never see clients. Younger lawyers are often the workhorses of the firm, buried in boxes of discovery responses and legal research. They get the lowliest of assignments, such as writing the firm blog. Yet, they seem to be motivated as they dream of gaining the label "partner" or "shareholder".

It is no wonder baby lawyers are discouraged, feel stuck due to law school debt, and get depressed before their career even launches.

Compassionate lawyers that start and finish well are strong and influential leaders

Lawyers are never taught basic leadership skills, yet we are thrown into leadership roles everywhere we go. Based on research, lawyers who finish well are likely to possess the following leadership characteristics: [4]

1. **They attend to their inner life to the end**
   The inner life involves a continual assessment to ensure one is "on target" with life. Lawyers must take the time to

reflect on their lives. Although it may be difficult due to busyness, it can be done during spiritual practices or solitude.

2. **They maintain a learning posture throughout life**
   What are lawyers doing to learn new skills that keep us sharp and passionate about our work? As part of the compassionate lawyer movement, we must expand the areas of knowledge for lawyers. Instead of learning about substantive topics that are lecture oriented, what about a wider variety of interesting seminars, such as healthy eating, leadership, communication skills, coaching and mentoring younger lawyers, skill building courses in empathy, and active listening? Can we make learning more diverse, perhaps via Continuing Legal Education (CLE)?

3. **They model strong character throughout life**
   There are times when we fall away from our character and integrity, whether it is a small deviation or a long detour. Many lawyers do whatever it takes to win a case, while very few encourage their client to "do the right thing." Compassionate lawyers encourage clients and define winning in a way that is broader than it has been in the past. For example as a family lawyer, I have always been intrigued when lawyers advocate for a client to pay minimal child support. If the earning parent pays no support, how will the children be supported? The idea of collaborative law has been instrumental in making sure that the entire family can survive financially. The collabora- tive concept considers ramifications of everyone involved rather than the particular client.

4. **They live their lives such that their beliefs are real in their lives and in their work**
   Lawyers who live with conviction live in courage as they stand up for their beliefs, even if their positions are unpopular. The members of the Iowa Supreme Court

who wrote the Varnum decision on gay marriage are a prime example, as they put their professional reputations on the line and lost their positions after re-election. Although some viewed the decision as unpopular, the Court was courageous.

Courageous and compassionate lawyers are assertive in the way they express themselves, making their point with clarity and listening to others who are doing the same. They do what they need to in order to honor their convictions.

5. **They contribute to the profession, making a mark and leaving a legacy**
Compassionate lawyers work to improve the quality of our field, investing in younger lawyers, and leaving legacies that will have a long-lasting effect.

As lawyers, we have case law on the books for cases we have handled. When you look back, as a lawyer, on reported cases bearing your name, consider whether your legacy is true to your character and your life's mission. Or are you one that likes the notoriety of a reported case? Will your grandchildren be proud of your legacy?

6. **They live their life with a growing sense of destiny**
I would invite you to take a quiet moment and write out the events that led you to the law. Who were the people that helped you get there? What were the life events that led you to law school? What doors opened or closed? In writing my spiritual autobiography, I clearly realized there were events that led me to law school. That singular exercise changed the way I looked at my life. It was clear that I was meant to be a lawyer. Once we look at the law as a destiny, and not just a profession, it revolutionizes the way we live our professional lives.

You may have concluded law is not your calling as you are unfulfilled and your heart is calling you to do something else with your life. Do you have the courage to chart your course outside the practice, taking the excellent lawyering skills you have learned to your next adventure?

A colleague of mine, uneasy with the practice of law, decided to leave the practice and follow a passion for cooking. He and his wife opened a store to sell spices, oils, and other cooking delicacies. He joked that most lawyers who came through the doors said they were "jealous." A few years after he opened the store, he dropped dead while taking his dog for a walk. At his funeral I took solace in knowing that before he died he found his passion and had the courage to live his truth.

For those choosing to revitalize their lives as a practicing lawyer, moving to compassion alongside a mentor or like-minded colleague can hold you accountable to stay the course and revitalize your life.

EVALUATION OF BLOWOUT, BURNOUT, AND PLATEAUING

The following questions are designed to help you identify if you suffer from Blowout, Burnout or Plateauing.

If any of these are happening to you, perhaps you are suffering from **Blowout**:

1. Are there aspects of your life that are secretive? For example do you have a secret relationship; do you use drugs; are you involved in pornography?

2. Are you rationalizing or justifying behaviors that you know deep down go against your integrity?

3. Do you have a loss of personal peace?

4. Do you have an accountability partner or partners or do you surround yourself with "yes men/women?"

5. Are you argumentative and insistent on having your own way?

6. When you are under pressure do you cut corners or take the path of least resistance?

7. Do you blame circumstances and others for your problems?

8. Do you tend to use people up rather than building them up?

9. Are you neglecting your primary relationships? (family, spouse, key leaders, staff)

10. Do you seek input from others of high integrity, or do you do things based on your own insights and methods?

If any of these are happening to you, perhaps you are suffering from **Burnout:**

1. Inconsistent connection to spirit, through spiritual practice, solitude, nature or other personal access points.

2. Regularly working long days without ability to manage schedule.

3. Inconsistent day off (at least once per week).

4. Lack of recreational interests and regular exercise (2-3 times per week).

5. Frequent fatigue, depression or discouragement (prone to sickness).

6. Lack of enjoyment in life, leadership, and profession (frequent thoughts of quitting).

7. Frequent friction with spouse and children (easily frustrated and angry).

8. Frequent friction with superiors, collegaues, staff (easily impatient and judgmental).

9. Growing numbers of uncompleted tasks, projects, missed appointments.

10. Disconnection with accountability partner or mentor, lack of accountability.

If any of these are happening to you, perhaps you are **Plateauing**:

1. Have a series of failures caused you to lose confidence and feel that you are more about self preservation?

2. Do you have a loss of assurance that your "calling" is to be a lawyer?

3. Have you lost passion and idealism for the practice and instead do you default to "keeping the peace" and "maintaining the status quo?"

4. Are you spending time dreaming about another relationship, position or promotion? Or maybe leaving the practice of law altogether?

5. Do you have a growing appetite for creature comforts or wealth as a sense of worth?

6. Is it difficult to make the tough decisions, or do you make them in a cavalier manner?

7. Is one of your top priorities covering your bases, taking care of your own needs first?

8. Have you become more cynical?

9. Have you become more critical or passive aggressive of other's creative, change oriented ideas especially if they mean change, loss of control or influence, or more work for you?

10. Are you staying at your current position even if you are unfulfilled because you don't know what to do next or are fearful of making a change?

11. Are you isolating from people who are moving forward and invigorated in the practice and instead hanging out with the veterans who are hanging on until retirement?

Chapter 9

Serving

Compassionate lawyers utilize their unique skills and wisdom in philanthropic endeavors

My Dad always told me he enjoyed being a lawyer because of the effect a lawyer has on others. The reason many of us go to law school is to "help people." Lawyers have strong abilities to communicate, persuade, and influence. If a lawyer sounds a call to action, others will likely follow. As lawyers, how are we utilizing our skills? Are we helping others outside of our legal practices? Are we inspiring other lawyers to do the same?

Lawyers dedicate their time, serving in leadership positions in various walks of life. We may sit on boards, run homeowners associations, coach little league, or rescue stray dogs from the ARL. But how are we using our lawyer skills, wisdom, and training specifically in serving others?

Maybe we are writing checks.

I vividly remember, as a young lawyer, a firm meeting where the senior partner reminded us it was time to sign up for pro bono month, designated by the Bar Association. "So everybody get out your checkbooks and write a check to Legal Aid," he said. Being young and too naïve to know better, I asked if it was possible to actually take some pro bono cases. "We prefer not because those are hours that impact your billable hour quota." Case closed.

Pro bono and reduced rate representation

Compassionate lawyers do more than write checks. They identify creative ways they can use their legal skills. The most obvious is to take a pro bono case. Although it seems easy, there are war stories about lawyers doing so to their detriment.

I once represented a pro bono client and hoped to settle her case, but we ended up in trial. She was not pleased with the outcome of the case. Disgruntled, she threatened to kill me. Literally. She also threatened to kill the head of the Volunteer Lawyer's Program. Later she filed a malpractice claim against me, which required me to call my malpractice insurance carrier.

Any malpractice claim or grievance, even if frivolous, causes a lawyer to lose sleep and doubt him or herself. In extreme circumstances, a lawyer may panic about his or her ability to survive in the event of getting reprimanded or even disbarred. To have a pro bono client file an unfounded malpractice claim was painful because I actually ended up paying with my soul and precious time for something that was supposed to be for a higher good.

Pro bono clients are often shut out of the legal system due to cost. Many have never met a lawyer in their life. When a lawyer chooses to take on a pro bono case, it is important to evaluate whether the client is a "legitimate" pro bono client. Where I practice, the Volunteer Lawyers Program bridged the gap between clients who are not eligible for pro bono, but cannot afford regular rates. The case administrator screens the client for eligibility. Clients who fall just short of qualifying for pro bono are offered a lawyer for $50/hour. Lawyers interested in pro bono sign up for the $50 rate. It's a great system, especially for young lawyers starting a solo practice as they get experience, deal with opposing counsel, and get paid something, all while doing a public service.

Boundaries revisited

Compassionate lawyers must set boundaries, as pro bono clients and their problems can become exhausting. I often connect with my pro bono clients in a way that I become an ongoing resource long after their case is over. This is likely true for other lawyers as well. Clients may seek our guidance throughout their lives. This can be rewarding as long as we set appropriate boundaries and recognize that they must respect our time. If we do not establish firm boundaries, clients may abuse our generosity. Understanding whether clients are highly motivated or whether they are taking advantage is a key to administering compassion.

Several years ago I represented a pro bono client who moved into her parent's house after living in a homeless shelter with her three children, one of which was an infant. She had a history of using meth, but with the help of treatment, she was trying to stay clean. We got her legal matters settled, divorcing her from the father of her two oldest children and granting her primary care. In another paternity case, we negotiated primary care of her infant to her baby's father with extraordinary visitation to her.

She stayed clean from drugs and enrolled in school, completing a two-year degree. She was studying to become a paralegal and helped me work on the documents for her child support contempt action when her children's father had stopped paying support. I had a front row seat to watching her reclaim her self-esteem and her life.

I served as her lawyer, but also as somewhat of a mentor. When she had to make an important decision she would call to run it by me. I would listen, be supportive, tell my thoughts, and always commend her on the progress she was making. The other thing I did, which was of huge value to her, was that I reminded her she was worthy, and that she was not her past. Her Dad also went back to school and the two of them competed for grades. When she called to report her grades, her Dad would also get on the phone so I could fawn over his efforts. Has she made some poor decisions since we have known each other? Absolutely. But she has come so far. I like to think that I helped her find her path just by shining a light on the road ahead of her.

I had another pro bono client that was an alcoholic and had some serious physical ailments. I helped her get alimony and keep joint legal custody of her kids. Her husband hired a "full pay" lawyer who would have taken everything away from her had she not been represented. I also contacted a social security disability lawyer for her. The case involved numerous hours of pro bono representation, attending a mediation, and drafting several documents – a time intensive case to be sure.

I recently got a call from her. She fell into a relapse, actively drinking and making many poor decisions, and she could not tell me whether she had followed through on the disability claim. Her ex-husband was trying to gain full custody of the children.

I sadly explained to her that I could not represent her a second time. She did not meet my required criteria for pro bono clients, which is they must be "highly motivated." I made a personal decision that with my own caseload and having helped her the first time, it was not appropriate to dive in again.

Instead I referred her to a young lawyer and told him if he represented her pro bono I would come to the initial consultation to provide background and strategize the next steps. He declined the representation. Was that the right decision? I don't judge. It was his call. As far as I know, this young lawyer had never taken a pro bono case.

I always tell lawyers, particularly young lawyers, that if they take a pro bono case it will come back to them tenfold. I have experienced it myself. It is not only self-satisfying, but it also results in increased business. It is as if the universe blesses one's effort to help the poor by bringing in more paying clients.

Most bar associations recognize lawyers who do a great deal of pro bono with luncheons and fancy certificates. For some reason, I have never felt that such recognition is appropriate. I dream of a day when every lawyer does one pro bono case per year without fanfare. Can you imagine the impact?

Legal aid

Taking cases is not the only form of pro bono work. Legal Aid is under-funded and understaffed. The phones ring off the wall and people are constantly walking in looking for a lawyer. I have, on occasion, volunteered for an afternoon serving as an intake lawyer at Legal Aid, talking to people and screening them for staff lawyers or doing immediate problem solving on the phone. Most of the time, in ten minutes or less, I could answer questions, treat the caller with a level of respect and dignity, exchange pleasantries with them and sometimes even reassure them of something to ease their anxiety. In one afternoon lawyers can have an impact on countless people's lives.

Youth in the community

When I moved back to Iowa I became involved in a middle school mentoring program. I was assigned a mentee, an African-American girl whom I will call Valencia. She was a 7th grade student. Her father was in prison, so her mother was working to support a large family. Valencia was having problems in school, but she was very smart.

My role, as a mentor, was to meet Valencia at her school for lunch once a week, listen to her, and take an interest in her. Due to Valencia's particular issues, I went beyond the scope of my job description. When she was ill, I'd pick her up from school, stop at the store for over-the-counter medicine, and give her a ride home. I met with the principal when she had a discipline problem. I took her to dinner and taught her table manners, introducing her to various types of foods. I attended several of her school plays. I also brought her to some of my family functions.

Valencia respected that I was a lawyer. We talked about education. I told her I would watch her grades closely and because I knew she was smart, I had high expectations. I took a strong interest in her academics.

Valencia and I were mentor/mentee through her high school years as well. She ended up getting a partial scholarship to a four-year university a few hours from her home. She was doing well until the summer before she left for college. She was picked up for shoplifting a clothing item and the prosecutor decided to charge her with a felony. Since I am not a criminal attorney, she was appointed a public defender.

Valencia's legal battle was stressful for everyone. Her mother called me and begged me to do something to get her out of jail. I was able to get calls back from her busy public defender, even though Valencia herself did not, and then I relayed the information to her family. With the permission of her defense lawyer I talked to the prosecutor, letting him know that I was her mentor and that I would like to make a statement on her behalf. "Does she know how lucky she is to have you?" the prosecutor asked. He took note of me as a lawyer friend on Valencia's side.

As her punishment, Valencia spent time in the county jail and had to serve time over her Christmas break when she was home from college. Her family could only see her on TV monitors in the lobby of the jail, if they were even able to get to the jail, because she was confined behind concrete walls. Who could visit her, sit with her, and touch her while she was in confinement? A lawyer.

I went to the jail, got in, and was able to meet with her in a little meeting room specially for lawyers and clients. I was able to hug her and hold her hand while we talked. "I will never be like the women in here," she told me. She told me that she mentioned to the other inmates she was heading to college and they laughed at her. We talked and prayed together and she could dissect things with her mentor, the lawyer.

Valencia was the first woman in her family to graduate from a four-year university.

Compassionate lawyers look around the world, outside of the office, and see where his or her lawyer skills can be utilized

Hospice

When my grandmother Josephine was dying of lung cancer, I was so impressed by the hospice care she received that I wanted to do something in return. When I offered, they asked me what special skills I had. I couldn't think of any but said "I am a lawyer." We came up with a plan, and I recruited my Dad and his law partner to join me in mobile will writing for indigent hospice patients.

The Hospice staff began asking poverty stricken patients if they needed a will. Technically, because they were indigent, they didn't need a will. But emotionally, they did. We went to patient bedsides and talked to them about their wills. When we calmly discussed their will, it often led to the family having their first open discussion about death. In many instances, the patient had been waiting to have the discussion, but it wasn't until the lawyer was present that there was a forum to do so.

We also prepared living wills, which always opened a discussion on the patient's feelings about life support. As a result of our work and our ability to talk with the dying party present, family members felt more empowered to make painful end-of-life decisions.

Most importantly, we sat by the bedsides and we listened attentively as hospice patients told their life stories. One woman pointed to each stuffed animal in an assortment and made sure I wrote down which grandchild got which stuffed animal. Some of the bequests were heart-wrenching. When we returned back to the bedsides later to execute the will, we brought our own family members or legal secretaries to serve as witnesses. Sometimes we notarized a signature so lightly written, due to weakness, that we debated whether it was adequate.

Tears often poured once we stepped outside the room. Who sat with these grieving families in their darkest hour? Compassionate lawyers and their compassionate staff members, using their unique skill and training in the legal profession.

I will never forget when a new client walked into my office during the years of that project, giving me a vast amount of legal work for himself and his small company. Delighted, I asked him how he had selected me. "My mother was a hospice patient and you came to her house and did her will for free," he said. "That is the kind of lawyer I want working for me."

Helping the elderly

A colleague of mine helps drivers over age 66 who are involved in a traffic accident and have their licenses revoked. In Iowa, the license is revoked, regardless of whether the elder was ticketed. The impact to these people, particularly in rural Iowa, can be devastating.

The compassionate lawyer told me, "When they see me walk in to the Department of Transportation office, wearing my suit, white shirt, and bright asymmetrical Italian or French tie, the behind-the-wheel inspector always passes my grateful client. I offer to drive my newly re-licensed client home, an offer which has always been accepted. I think I now know how immigration guides felt at Ellis Island."

Educating the public

At the Iowa State Fair, the young lawyers division of the Iowa Bar Association recruits volunteers to work in a booth that provides legal information and resources. Over 100 attorneys usually volunteer to hold down a three hour shift at some point in the fair.

From the Iowa Bar Association website: "The goal of the committee is to educate and inform the public about our jury and legal system. The committee plans, organizes, and coordinates a mock trial that is presented each night at the Iowa State Fair. Members of the Fair audience are chosen to act as jury members. Following the mock trial there is a question and answer period. Committee members help raise funds to put on the event, write or select cases to be used for the mock trial, coordinate judges, lawyers, court reporters and witnesses for each night at the fair and act as a moderator at least one night at the fair."[1]

Immigration clinic

My Greek Orthodox church in Iowa had an influx of immigrants from Africa. They were all indigent, learning English and had no understanding of the immigration system. An immigration lawyer in our parish set up an immigration clinic one Sunday and brought her secretary to help. I assisted in filling out paperwork, even though I don't have a clue about immigration law. We ran the clinic all afternoon. The compassionate lawyer and her secretary took the documents back to the firm, finishing the immigration process for free.

American Mock Trial Association

Few people know that the American Mock Trial Association was formed in Iowa. The actual tournament was formed by my long time office mate Richard (Dick) Calkins, when he was the Dean of the Drake University Law School. Dick was joined by my father Dan Stamatelos, former Iowa Chief Justice Ward Reynoldson, and another attorney colleague Gene Reifsnider, to form the first board of the organization. All of these compassionate lawyers served the organization for free, often digging into their own pockets to keep it going in the early years.

Mock trial has expanded to high school, junior high, and even elementary school competitions. These competitions always need lawyers to help judge. Imagine how the feedback of an interested compassionate lawyer could impact a bright eyed lawyer-to-be.

Thousands of young people have been involved in mock trial since its inception. Some participants go to law school, while others will work in policymaking and government. Either way, participants experience the difficult and complicated job of the lawyer up close and personal. They gain a respect for what lawyers do. Can you imagine the legacy of the compassionate lawyers who started this organization?

Guest speakers

I think one would be hard pressed to find a teacher or professor that

167

didn't want a lawyer to speak to their students. While I was in Arizona, I spoke at my son's elementary school for career day. I was on the speaking circuit with a chef from a fancy resort, as well as others with exotic careers. I was explaining the job of mediator. Taking a cue from the popular book, *"Getting to Yes"* by Fisher and Ury,[2] I brought an orange for my presentation. I asked my son and another classmate to come up and fight over the orange. They rejoiced in their moment of drama. I split the orange in half and gave it to them. I explained that my son wanted to eat the "fruit" of the orange and his classmate wanted the peel for a fruitcake recipe. I showed them that if I had listened to their interests and needs, I could have peeled the orange and provided each with double the amount they'd gotten by simply cutting it in half. "Splitting the baby" hadn't resulted in the best outcome.

I don't know if my young son or any of his classmates understood the concept, but the chef came up to me after to ask more about mediation because he was in the middle of a dispute at the time. As lawyers, we never know how the information we present at speeches or meetings across the country will affect others.

Consulting on school programs

I once read about playground mediation programs in some of my professional literature. I ordered some materials and approached my children's school about setting up a peer mediation program for the playground. Lawyers can identify conflict and justice issues every-where we turn if we are awake to the idea of service as lawyers, even at places as unsuspecting as the elementary playground.

Compassionate programs

Attorney Fred Van Liew is a wonderful example of how a lawyer can use compassion to change the culture in any legal job you may hold.[3]

Fred was hired by the Polk County Iowa Attorney's office in 1984 as a prosecutor. Frustrated that he could not follow his heart's desire to do pro bono work as a government lawyer, he started Government

Attorneys Resisting Poverty (GARP). The program was later renamed Government Attorneys Pro Bono (GAP).

Van Liew put together an advisory board that encouraged volunteer lawyers to respond to the need for alternative dispute resolution. With the assistance of mediator Mike Thompson, lawyers participated in a two-day training. During the training a film was shown, demonstrating the use of victim-offender mediation in a criminal case. The video showed a woman in her 30's who, along with her young daughters, were victims of a home invasion perpetrated by a 16 year-old offender. The victims spoke of how the offender's actions impacted their life and personal sense of security. Hearing this, the offender cried, "I never knew that I had caused such harm."

While Fred watched the video, he said, "Something opened up in me. I didn't know what to do with this recognition of the very human need for victims and offenders to engage in dialogue." He continued his work as a prosecutor for another year without the question being answered.

Fred left the prosecutor's office, but later returned to the Polk County Attorney's office in 1991 as the Bureau Chief of Intake and Screening on the criminal side. At that time, the County Attorney's office managed the Neighborhood Mediation Center, which utilized community mediators to handle minor offenses and disputes. Fred was spurred by an inner stirring of compassion and recognized the power of a safe place to tell one's story, so he began to investigate Restorative Justice. He bought 20 copies of Howard Zehr's "*Changing Lenses*" and gave one to each of the neighborhood mediators. Then he brought in Mark Umbreit, a Restorative Justice expert from the University of Minnesota, who trained mediators to facilitate victim-offender dialogues. This initiated a shift, allowing the mediators to facilitate matters less from a punishment perspective, but more from an accountability perspective.

The program opened the door to the community of criminal defense attorneys but many were skeptical. Public defenders, however, were quicker to accept the process, hoping it would result in a change of heart for their clients and possibly reduce recidivism. Van Liew recalls that when lawyers accompanied their clients to the mediated dialogues, they were transformed as they observed "the miracle is in the process and that, while education is important, more important is being in the meeting, holding the pain with the participants, and watching healing happen right before your eyes." Judges were also initially skeptical, saying "lawyers should not engage in social work." As time went on, however, judges saw the value of victim-offender meetings, routinely ordering offenders to participate in the process, both in criminal and juvenile cases.

Because of the success of the program, the County Attorney's office established a Restorative Justice Center funded by the County Board of Supervisors. The Center has grown over the years, now employing a program manager and several full-time non-lawyer staff. Employees prepare the victims and offenders to meet one another, as well as discuss the harm caused by the offender and how that harm can be repaired through offender accountability.

Van Liew further created the first domestic abuse docket in the state, as well as several other Restorative Justice programs. In addressing the issues surrounding domestic abuse, he met with people in the victim community to identify both the legal and psychological training needs for prosecutors and police, so they can more effectively and compassionately work with victims.

Fred has left the county attorney office to pursue his passion of conflict resolution and to train others in Restorative Justice practices, victim-offender meetings remain important in the process of administering justice in Polk County. Most recently, Fred was instrumental in developing a Court Watch program in Des Moines, Iowa. Volunteers are recruited to politely, respectfully, and quietly observe what justice looks like in our juvenile courts, as juvenile court reforms are being explored.

Beginner's mind

I have been a practitioner of yoga since my freshman year of college. One of the beautiful yoga philosophies, borrowed from Zen Buddhism, is the concept of beginner's mind. This concept encourages one to have an attitude of openness, eagerness, and a lack of preconceptions toward a subject. It is the ability to see something just as a beginner would.

In context, for yogis and yoginis, it may mean that although we are doing our one millionth downward facing dog, we embrace it as though it was our very first. For lawyers, it may mean when meeting clients we hearken back to meeting our first client or having our first experience as a lawyer. As an adjunct professor of law, surrounded by young law students, I have a front row seat to beginner's mind.

In the mediation course I teach, we conclude with a "mediation day." With the cooperation of the Volunteer Lawyers Program we have about seven cases going at once, every three hours. The students co-mediate cases for indigent clients living in poverty who participate pro se (without lawyers representing them). Most of the cases involve divorce, child support, or other family issues. The students mediate while I circulate, supervising, and answering legal questions. At the conclusion of the mediation, the clients choose whether to have a lawyer review the mediation agreement before they sign, or they can sign a waiver of further legal representation and sign the mediation agreement.

Our Volunteer Lawyers Program finds that more lawyers will volunteer to shepard legal documents through the system in a divorce if all the issues have already been resolved in a mediation agreement because their volunteer work is simply administrative, rather than full blown representation. This project is a win-win for the students, the pro bono attorneys, and the clients.

I tell students before our big day that they are more than likely the only lawyer that these clients will ever meet. Certainly they may be the only lawyer who has all the time in the world to sit with the client. I remind them that the impression they make in that moment they meet the client will mark indelibly how those people feel about lawyers.

The response I get from students amazes me every year. They all show up decked to the nines in suits and ties, or skirts. What was surprising to me is that most of the students admitted to never having any personal exposure to someone living in poverty.

One student reported that a party had just been released from prison and come straight to the mediation. Another student was shocked that a husband showed up to resolve a divorce with his pregnant girlfriend, and that the husband, wife, and pregnant girlfriend all got along. Students always find what many pro bono lawyers know: people in poverty often get along better in complicated circumstances than people of means.

One student came to me saying she needed to sit quietly for a moment, and when she did, she teared up. She was overwhelmed that a mom, who was a drug user, admitted that she could not stay clean. The mother wanted to sign documents ensuring that her children would be safe because she was fairly certain she would die at some point from drug overdose. She also did not want to be able to get access to the kids if she was using. The student was in awe of the courage, the sense of hopelessness, and the fact that as a lawyer-to-be, she could somehow assure this wounded woman that her babies would be protected.

Most of the students were invigorated by the experience. Almost all of them, in their term papers, stated that they want to do pro bono work. I don't know how many of them will, but I'd venture to say that there is a higher probability after getting a taste of what it felt like in their mediation experience. Some excerpts from their papers:

"I learned a great deal during this mediation course. Probably the most significant thing I learned was the true worth of being an attorney; to serve as an advocate for those who need a voice. The skills and methodologies of client communication I learned during this process will serve me greatly in the future in my transactional practice. Be open and honest with your clients and never hide the ball from them. Set expectations for them from the very beginning. Not unrealistic expectations; expectations they can believe in. And above all, listen to them. Listen to their needs, be empathetic of their needs, and give them the audience they need and deserve. To put it another way, in the words of our professor, "everyone just wants to feel loved." – *Michael*

"I also enjoyed the feeling of helping the clients in the VLP. Hearing how long some of them had been waiting to get a divorce troubled me. I hope that once I'm in practice I will have enough time to really be able to give back and help those who are less fortunate. I plan on continuing to mediate for the VLP while I'm in school." – *Sam*

"While it is important to understand the law behind everything we will end up doing, it is also important to have a class which focuses on how to interact with clients and how to help them in a human way. I've only had one other class which has even broached the topic of how to get a client to talk to you. The clients are coming to you in the worst time of their lives and often telling you things they aren't comfortable discussing. Knowing how to get them to speak with you and feel comfortable is the only way that an attorney can adequately represent a client and truly get them what they want and need." – *Megan*

(Referring to the professor) "As someone who has given me hope that being a lawyer does not require ruthlessness or merciless advocacy. Rather, she has shown by example that the legal profession can still serve to help people." – *Susan*

"It was, honestly, the first time in my life I have sat down and spoken at length to people using drugs, suffering abuse, receiving state welfare, and getting by without one dime to their names. At times, it was hard to extrapolate myself from their lives and focus on reaching resolution, and not subconsciously push for an outcome that I felt was best based on my own reasoning or moral judgments. Perhaps what struck me the most is that I fully expected one or more people at some point to stop and ask me what the heck I knew when making suggestions and working through their issues. I felt like I was just a law student with a little legal experience and far less life experience telling people older than me, with families and real problems, how to proceed with major life decisions. I was sure someone would challenge our credentials or dismiss us. But everyone listened appreciatively to what (co-mediator student) and I proposed, and never once objected to our knowledge or abilities. I know that they needed us to obtain a court-required service, but I also got the sense that they truly did appreciate our help and took us seriously (whether or not we felt like we were truly qualified). Some clients just needed someone to hear them, to take the time to discuss their concerns, and at the end of the process they seemed to trust us. In that, it was a rewarding and empowering experience in an unexpected way. This course has taught me the importance of pro bono and volunteer work once I am a licensed attorney." – *Becky*

"This class also showed me how valuable volunteer work can be. Just spending a few hours can make all the difference in the world to people who need help with their legal problems, but cannot afford to hire a private attorney. Mediating the cases in this class also gave me a great sense of accomplishment for helping these people out. I look forward to doing mediations and volunteer work going forward in my legal career." – *Jonathan*

"Overall, this class was an extremely positive experience. It was very interesting and difficult taking the lawyer cap off and putting on the mediator cap. It made me realize how much law schools train students to think a certain way, and it is really difficult to break that habit. The lawyer cap is much more impersonal and outcome oriented. When thinking like a lawyer it is easy to lose touch with the fact that you are dealing with people who have their own feelings and futures to worry about. When wearing the lawyer cap I am more often concerned with formulating arguments, attacking the other party's argument, devising a strategy and "winning" the case. The mediator cap is much more personal and cordial. It reminded me that treating people with respect and helping them through a difficult time in their life is more important than "winning" anything. For a mediator, winning is not a personal thing. Winning means treating both sides with respect while doing your best to come up with creative ways to help them reach a solution so they can move on with their lives. In this respect mediation is more fulfilling than the work I have done as a law clerk. Mediation allows you to really see and feel the effect you are having on people's lives, which was the most enjoyable part of the process for me." – *Corey*

"In the near future, I am hoping to get involved with the Volunteer's Lawyer Project and help with mediations in Polk County. I have been in contact with VLP and so am just waiting until they need my help." – *Rebecca*

These students remind us why we entered the law. Most of us came to the field so we can "help people" and most of us knew that we wanted to make a difference.

What could happen?

What would happen if, instead of simply writing a check, each lawyer took one pro bono case a year or found one way to use their legal expertise in a unique way? It might just awaken a sleeping compassion gene that got lost in the frenzy of law firm life. Am I overestimating the potential impact when I tell you I believe the service of compassionate lawyers could change the world?

Chapter 10

Fair and Just

Compassionate lawyers establish fair and just billing practices and have a healthy relationship with money

I'll bet everyone has heard some variation of the following joke:

> *A lawyer died and went to heaven, where he met St. Peter at the Pearly Gates.*
>
> *"I see you lived to the ripe old age of 210," St. Peter said to him.*
>
> *"No, I died of a heart attack at 67," the lawyer said.*
>
> *"Well," St. Peter said, "we calculated your age based on billable hours."*

Billable hours may be the most stressful topic for all lawyers. This area is one where even a compassionate lawyer comes face-to-face with character and conviction on literally, an hourly basis.

New and young lawyers, especially in firms, are expected to prove their worthiness by the number of hours they bill. It is the primary way their superiors value them.

When I joined my first firm in the 1980's, I was working long arduous hours, but still came up short on my billable hour quota. I didn't know what to do, so I sought advice from one of the partners. He told me,

"Just come in, write down the matters you are working on, figure out how many hours you were here in the office, and divide up the total hours you were working somehow amidst those matters." At the end of our conversation I was even more troubled as his advice seemed inherently unfair both to clients and to me.

Some days later, I went to lunch with another young associate and we discussed my dilemma about billable hours. He inquired as to the status of various matters I was working on and I regaled him with stories about my cases for the rest of our lunch break. As we finished, he scratched the names on the back of a napkin and said, "I'm billing each client you described for the time in our discussion here at lunch. That's how you do it."

Billable hour quotas are the hallmark of many lawyers' lives. In most firms it is the measurement stick for compensation increases, partnership distinction, and general notoriety in the firm. As my legal career progressed, I realized that with billable hour quotas I am virtually behind the minute I hit the door, even if I arrive as the sun comes up.

The problem with this paradigm is that it only focuses on making money rather than providing compassion and quality service to the clients; it encourages overdoing legal matters, misusing legal discovery, and taking unnecessary steps in order to "churn" a case. It is difficult to have a clear focus on what needs to be done, because the lawyer may view the client as a billable opportunity instead of a human being.

One of the main reasons I left the law firm environment and became a solo practitioner was to have the freedom to bill clients fairly. In a case I am currently working on, my client told me that she and her soon to be ex-husband were comparing their divorce lawyer bills. They noticed her husband's lawyer bills $140 for every email exchange with me, but those emails are not showing up on my bill to her. I didn't have the heart to tell her the content of the emails are trivial, such as "My client got ahold of the appraiser and they will begin the appraisal next Monday," and my exchange is "Sounds good, thanks."

How do compassionate lawyers reconcile this issue?

Fee agreements

Any lawyer knows one must have a fee agreement with the client before undertaking work. Both the client and the lawyer sign the fee agreement. But what's in the fee agreement?

Some fee agreements are long and complicated. I'd venture to say that most clients do not fully understand the language used in a standard attorney fee contract. Not only that, but the client is often signing the fee agreement after the consultation with the attorney, at a time when he or she is emotionally distraught. At such a time, the client often trusts the lawyer to simply take care of the matter.

The client usually just wants to know what he or she owes in order to get the ball rolling. Rarely does the client know the intricacies of how the lawyer charges because he or she does not have the ability to calmly and completely read the fee agreement and understand it.

Is it appropriate to encourage a client to sign up right at the conclusion of the consultation? Unless there is a matter of urgency, it may be best to give the client time to reflect before signing up for representation. Give the client a chance to take the fee agreement home, read it, discuss it with a loved one, or even compare it to other lawyers'. I often tell clients who are "lawyer shopping" to be sure to review the fee agreement with the lawyer they see next and to be sure they understand what they are paying for.

When clients do ask to retain me right after a consultation, I will go over the fee agreement slowly with them, making sure they understand every sentence. My fee agreement is on one page. I tell them to call me, at no charge, if they have any questions regarding their bill. There are certainly lawyers who bill clients for calls regarding their bill.

I recently met with an intellectual property lawyer over matters pertaining to this book. She is an incredibly compassionate lawyer in a big firm. As I explained the compassionate lawyer concepts and game plan to her, she was enthused and listened intently. At the end of my consultation, I said, "You probably have a fee agreement for me that is three or more pages long with a lot of big words, and if I weren't a lawyer, I probably would not understand it." She sheepishly pulled a document exactly as I described out of her pile of notes and looked it over, nodding.

As an aside, when I went for the consultation, it was at a time when I had cut my practice back in order to work on this book. My income had taken a substantial decrease. The entire time I was attending the consultation, I was mindful of my time and was worried about what she would charge. I realized I had not clarified the cost of the consult and I was too embarrassed to ask.

When I offered to pay her at the conclusion of our 90 minutes, she said, "There is no charge as a professional courtesy to you and to help you move this project forward." I was so happy, I actually started to get tears in my eyes. I felt, first hand, what impact a compassionate lawyer can have on their potential clients.

A compassionate lawyer has a short and succinct fee agreement. It is written in layman's terms that the client can understand. When entering into a retaining agreement with a client, the lawyer should read the contract alongside the client, explaining the terms and watching to be sure the client is following. The lawyer also sends a copy with the client for his or her later reference at the conclusion of the meeting.

Recently a close friend lost a job when she was fired by her employer, three weeks after turning age 65. I helped her find and retain an employment attorney to assist her in what we believe is an actionable claim of age discrimination and I went with my friend to the meetings with her lawyer. A fee agreement was never offered and I repeatedly asked for one. I did not get it until the third meeting. When I got it, the fee structure was set out incorrectly. After I pointed it out to the lawyer, we finally got a corrected fee agreement. I wondered what might have happened if I had not been in the meetings. I know that my friend was so distraught over her unemployment status she could not hear anything the lawyer was saying, and most certainly didn't understand the complicated fee shifting provisions of employment law. Ultimately I sat down and explained them to her outside the meeting with her lawyer and told her that she could sign the fee agreement once she understood.

Retainers

Retainers can be complicated, so it is important for the client to understand how they work. Retainers are deposits paid in advance and put in the lawyer's trust account. The lawyer bills monthly and then pulls amounts out of the retainer deposit to cover the monthly bills. Unused sums are refunded to the client at the conclusion of the case.

Lawyers are obligated to act as a fiduciary to the trust account, pulling funds only when earned or when otherwise in compliance with specific rules, usually set by the Supreme Court in the state where the lawyer practices. Best practices involve monthly detailed bills showing the amount of the retainer removed to pay the bill and providing the remaining balance.

Informing the client of how retainers are handled and that retainers are scrutinized by the supreme court or governing body, helps the client understand that the lawyer has a duty to be ethical when removing money from the trust account. I actually tell my clients, when explaining the trust account, that there is an auditor who stops by unexpectedly to audit my account. I also emphasize that, at the conclusion of the legal matter, I have to refund any fees not earned during my legal representation.

Do lawyers actually refund unused retainers? Or are there mysterious entries, such as "file closing" or "administrative" that eat up the lingering trust proceeds? When a lawyer has fees in hand or even in a trust account, it may be tempting to not refund the client. It amazes me the number of clients who are shocked they actually got money back from their lawyer at the end of their case.

Some firms use evergreen trust accounts, meaning there is a minimum balance required in the trust account at all times. When the balance gets down to the minimum amount, the client must replenish. Sometimes the entire trust account is an evergreen account. The client pays as the case goes on and the retainer is used as a "backup" security plan for the lawyer to get paid. If the evergreen fund is not used, the money is refunded. Clients may not understand these complexities. Fee agreements should spell out when new retainers will be requested. As compassionate lawyers we must point out, in the fee agreement, that replenishment is possible so clients can plan to do so if the case requires it.

One of the main reasons lawyers lose their license to practice law is due to the misuse of their trust account. Imagine you are a layperson with debt and you have a big pot of money sitting in your personal savings account. To pay your debt, you would likely just dip into the savings account. Lawyers, however, cannot use their trust account as a "savings account." The temptation of dipping into the trust account creates problems for some lawyers as they "borrow" from their trust account and repay it, or they just plain rob their trust account. Lawyers who unethically do this often get disbarred and get a claim against their security fund in order to repay it. One of my friends from law school, an excellent lawyer, lost his license for this reason. Even though he paid the trust account back with interest, his actions cost him his license.

Unbundled represenation

Not all legal relationships involve retainers. In some jurisdictions there is unbundled legal representation, meaning that the lawyer charges to do only a specific task for the client. It may be drafting a document, reviewing a contract, consulting on a special legal matter, giving a second opinion, or something that requires a limited amount of time. Many lawyers will charge for these types of projects on a "pay when completed" basis.

Hourly rate

What is an appropriate hourly rate for attorneys to charge? I recently talked to a young lawyer who just passed the bar and is setting up a solo practice doing work for other lawyers. With the possible exception of a clinical class in law school, the lawyer has no experience. When I asked the lawyer what his hourly rate was, he replied with a dollar figure that was commensurate to lawyers with five or more years experience.

I told the young lawyer I thought the proposed rate based on no experience was excessive. The young lawyer told me very directly that he thought he was absolutely worth that amount. Clients often have the perception that lawyers who charge more are worth more. The client is in for a rude awakening when this lawyer starts to handle their case.

Conversely, another highly experienced lawyer I interviewed continues to raise his hourly rate so that it is well above the high end of fees in town. He told me, "The more I raise my rate the more clients I get. I intend to keep raising it until my business drops off, but it hasn't happened yet, so I don't know where the ceiling is for my fee yet."

Unfortunately, because clients are beholden to us and don't know what we do exactly, they have no choice but to pay us whatever we charge. Sometimes it's only after the case that they find out whether they got quality legal service.

A lawyer's hourly rate is not necessarily commensurate with his or her skill. Charging the lowest rate in town doesn't make you a compassionate lawyer. In fact, most compassionate lawyers I know are on the higher end of the hourly rate spectrum. The difference, however, is that the clients get value. Value entails a problem solver and someone who is listening and working hard for them, rather than a lawyer who walks out of the consult, hands the file to a junior associate or paralegal, and then never talks to the client again.

Billing for support staff and junior lawyers

Most lawyers have support staff to some extent. It may be a legal assistant, a junior associate attorney, a secretary, or a law clerk/law student.

The support staff often does work on a client's file at a different bill-able rate than the lawyer.

Compassionate lawyers hire and train compassionate support staff. The rates charged by these staff members are fair and just. Compassionate lawyers introduce their support staff to the client and explain the role they will have on the client's case. The lawyer also makes the client feel comfortable with the qualifications of the staff person. After all, the client hires the lawyer, not the staff person. If other lawyers or staff will be handling pivotal parts of the client's case, they should be involved in the lawyer/client discussions so they have some background. Lawyers must make it clear to clients when they will respond to the client's requests and when their support staff will respond. Clients don't want the lawyer to disappear once they are retained, without explanation.

Another issue that clients must know and understand is which partic-ular attorneys are working on their matter. It's not an uncommon prac-tice for a senior partner rainmaker to woo the client to the signing of a fee agreement only to pass the file to an inexperienced associate, and then never see the client again. The senior lawyer can delegate the work, but must be clear to the client on expectations.

Clients should also understand the difference in billing rates for the support staff. This should also be explained in the fee agreement. When I was a younger lawyer, a legal assistant who was helping me learn to keep track of billable hours told me her prior boss had taken her billable hour tally and told her to enter all of her time in under his rate. The bill would reflect that the lawyer had done the work, when in reality the assistant had done it.

Using support staff needs to be appropriate under the circumstances. Lots of firms assign more than one lawyer or staff person to an assign-ment so a whole cluster of people is billing the client. This leads to duplicative billing, which clients don't detect or understand.

We must also consider whether it is a compassionate lawyer's obligation to inform clients when another attorney or paralegal can handle parts of their legal matter at a lower cost. Should we give the client the option of choosing representation from the younger associate if it is appropriate? Or do we bill at our higher rate for basic legal work that could have been delegated? At a minimum, do we owe it to our clients to let them know when an option is available?

I have found clients are grateful for these options. Sometimes they want the younger and less experienced lawyer and sometimes they tell me they want me to do all the work.

As for support staff billing, most clients don't have the discernment to know the difference between a lawyer, a law clerk, a legal secretary, a paralegal, or a summer intern. In some firms, every human in the office has a billable rate to the client for work done. Does the client know and understand this? I have had clients offer to make copies, collate documents, or hand deliver packages to other lawyers to save money. While there is a point at which this is inappropriate, is it really wrong to let a client step in like that to reduce cost? Or is it easier to tell the client that those tasks, the majority of which are done by support staff, are included in the hourly rate charge?

Some firms bill for every copy, fax, phone call, and other administrative cost while still billing their hourly rate. Does the client understand this? Is it fair? Is it more appropriate to bill for those items separately or to have a solid hourly billing rate that includes those items? Most compassionate lawyers feel a solid hourly rate is "all inclusive" as it is easier for the client.

Some lawyers charge for their elaborate overhead. They may have expansive offices, large numbers of support staff, and beautiful surroundings for clients. Some even have televisions or phenomenal electronics in each lawyer's office. Do clients like to pay for this? Most do not. Keep in mind that clients are coming to the "red cross tent" when they are wounded by legal matters. Are they more comfortable in a mausoleum or a warm, inviting space?

The biggest and brightest firms are not necessarily the best, but they are almost always the most expensive. On the other hand, smaller "boutique firms" can include amazing lawyers who recognize clients are looking for efficiency and customer service. They are less often concerned about the trappings. Lawyers looking to make their billing rates more affordable should determine whether their overhead can be streamlined.

Contingent fees

Clients rarely understand contingent fees. These fees mean the lawyer takes a percentage of what is recovered, so there is seemingly no cost if there is no recovery. The specifics, as far as costs and the lawyer's contingent proportion, can be confusing. A compassionate lawyer will not only explain the fee agreement, but may go through scenarios to show various recovery figures.

Clients also may not understand that they have a chance of a zero recovery. It is hard for lawyers to enlighten clients to this fact when, at the same time, they want to appear as though they are fighting for the client. To fail to apprise the client of this possibility is harmful to the client. It is crucial to inform clients that they will still be responsible for out of pocket costs, even when they get no monetary recovery.

As settlement opportunities come across the table, clients may decide they want to settle "to be done with it." A problem arises when the lawyer is in a joint venture with the client (because they are getting a piece of the action) and that lawyer may realize that a bigger recovery is possible if they go to trial. This conflict of interest can be problematic if the lawyer doesn't want to settle. Does the lawyer convince the client that they should roll the dice with the jury because they have a vested interest?

The same tension may occur with class action suits. Parties may sign up, only to receive a coupon for something trivial at the end of it all, yet the lawyers made an inordinate amount of fees as part of the settlement. This system is the source of many debates as to whether lawyers are the only ones getting a fair deal. As a compassionate lawyer, it is essential that we explain to our clients what they may expect, realistically, at the conclusion of a class action suit. Without clarity, clients may believe they will have a financial windfall coming to them.

Value billing

Value billing is when clients are charged based on the total value of services provided to the client rather than the amount of time it takes. For example, the lawyer may have developed very tightly worded documents in a prior case that only require some "tweaking" in the current case. Should the second client get the benefit of the documents initially drafted at the cost of another client? Most lawyers feel it is appropriate to charge for the value of having that previously drafted document available in subsequent matters.

Value billing can also be flat fee billing so that the fee is set between the lawyer and the client based on consideration for the scope of the work and expectations of the client. An example is to charge a flat fee for preparation of a will or a power of attorney. In these instances it is critical to have a clear understanding of what the client is buying for the set fee. In family law cases for example, repeated emails often drive up the bill. Clients that are limited to a specific number of emails should have a clear understanding of how the lawyer will respond to excessive or lengthy emails, if there is a response at all.

Statutory attorney's fees

Statutory fees are those established by state law. In certain types of action (such as employment disputes) there is a right to recover statutory attorney's fees if you win the case. This is dependent on the amount of time, labor, skill of the attorney, and difficulty of the issues among other factors.

Lawyers are allowed a percentage of the estate for handling the probate of an estate. Therefore, an attorney does not bill by the hour; regardless which attorney you hire, the fees are the same because the law has established the amount. Clients should be advised of this, and also understand what they might be required to pay and under what circumstances they might recover fees.

Clients may also have the right to recover attorney's fees as set forth in a contract. Again, they must understand that the right to collect does not ensure collectability.

Double billing

It is possible that clients get double billed. Lawyers can be loose with duplicating effort, often resulting in excessive charges to the client. I remember as a young lawyer when I worked side-by-side with a senior associate on a case and he told me, "Don't worry about what you are billing, we will review and write off your excessive time because of the learning curve." In fact, I heard that more than once. As I reviewed my bills, I found that the client was double billed for my time and the time of the senior lawyer who helped me on the project. Fair to the client?

Fee disputes

Younger lawyers who second chair senior lawyers at trial are another controversial area of billing. In my county, the bar association fee arbitration committee receives complaints from clients who feel they have been unjustly billed. The client registers a complaint and obtains a hearing in front of the committee. As a member of this committee, I read the complaints and attend the hearings on the fee disputes.

In one case, a layperson brought a grievance to the committee for alleged overcharging by his former lawyer on a small case. His trial was three days and two lawyers billed for all three days. At the hearing, the client questioned the junior lawyer, who second chaired, "Isn't it true that in three days you only asked two questions and yet you billed me for all three days?" "I don't recall how many questions I asked," replied the junior lawyer. Even the trial judge, in his written opinion cited "overstaffing" for that particular matter.

I am always amazed when lawyers let such fee grievances get to the level of a hearing before the committee. Even more painful is when an arrogant lawyer cross-examines the self-represented client who simply wanted to understand the bill, especially when the client probably would have paid it or accepted a modest write-off. The lawyer only re-wounds the client.

Most clients scoff at the idea of a group of lawyers deciding when other lawyers overcharge. (It must seem to the client like the foxes are in charge of the hen house.) Would these committees be served better by having laypersons in the midst, even in an advisory capacity? Could laypersons help us improve our ability to convey the intricacies and fairness of our billing system to our clients?

Clients who don't pay

Lawyers also have occasional issues in collecting fees from clients. So, what are appropriate boundaries for the compassionate lawyer? Can we sue our clients for fees? Should we? We have the right to do so, and our contractual agreement with the client may reinforce this. Is it the right thing for a compassionate lawyer to do?

Some lawyers have payment plans for clients. I remember my Dad would bring home jewelry and other personal items from clients who wanted to make payment on their bill. Clients may even have skills they can barter. While it may not be desirable, it can be better than a bad debt or a write-off. It also allows the client to uphold his or her dignity in being able to pay.

Although undesirable, there is always the option to write-off the debt or to have the "if you pay me now I will write-off part of this" attitude. However, much of this can be avoided by simply managing retainers as the case progresses. Checking in with the client can also help manage payment problems.

Some lawyers may also hold the release of final documents hostage or refrain from finalizing matters while billing is being sorted out. Is this compassionate?

Most jurisdictions allow lawyers to withdraw from cases if the client is not paying them. Clients also need to be aware of this and to hear it from the lawyer at the beginning of representation. If it is not covered in the oral review of the fee agreement, a client may feel blindsided when the lawyer later takes action. My experience is that clients who are informed are respectful and understand that a good lawyer needs to be paid.

How far can a lawyer go?

One woman shared her nightmare billing experience with me. She hired a lawyer because her ex-husband was allowing their young son to watch inappropriate R-rated films, drink sugar all the time, and play video games with violence. She requested the lawyer file something so her ex would have to go to counseling or parenting classes. The lawyer convinced her that she needed to file a modification of custody and charged her a handsome retainer, which was quickly used up.

The client never fully understood what a modification was, but there were volumes of documents being exchanged. The lawyer called midstream and asked for another retainer, three times more than the prior retainer. The client only received a few invoices, but trusted that the lawyer had spent the money wisely, even though no results seemed to be happening.

The parties and lawyers went to mediation where the ex-husband proposed settlement. The lawyer spoke sternly to the woman client, telling her that her ex-husband was obviously a sociopath and that the lawyer had a legal duty to persevere to change custody. The lawyer also told the client that without the legal intervention, the client should fear for her safety because the ex was the type that could hurt or kill her.

Terrified, the client borrowed money from a cousin, who questioned the lawyer's advice. The client had recently lost both of her parents, and the lawyer, a man her father's age, seemed trustworthy.

After mediation, motions were filed, but the client had no clarity of what was really going on. When she asked the lawyer why the money was eroding so quickly, the lawyer said "Well you call me all the time and use me as a counselor, too." Reporting that he had gotten the judge to order psych evaluations, the client had to give money to the lawyer's counselor friend to do a psychiatric evaluation of the ex-husband. The client also had to submit to a psych evaluation. The lawyer quoted one price for the psych evaluation, but the bill showed a payment to the counselor for only half the price.

As trial approached, the client ran out of funds and complained to the lawyer how much things were costing. The lawyer said that the client could pay $100 a month going forward until the time of trial. The client was so grateful she sent a thank you email to the lawyer saying "God bless you." Meanwhile, the lawyer told the client to withhold visitation of the child from her ex-husband because he was continuing to allow the child's behaviors that originated the lawsuit.

The Friday before the Monday trial, the woman client received a call in the evening from the attorney who said he had been so focused on the case that he had not noticed the client was negative $10,000 and that he could not go to trial unless he had the $10,000 by the following morning. If he didn't have the money he told the client that he would not show up at the courthouse Monday morning and the client would have to represent herself.

The client went to her banker the following morning and they told her that it would take two weeks to get the money. When the client started to cry the banker told her the lawyer story sounded fishy. The client, sobbing, called her best friend who had the personal cell phone number of a compassionate lawyer. The compassionate lawyer called the woman client, and told her not to give the lawyer another dime and to send an email, stating she knew the lawyer would show up on Monday morning with 100% effort, and that she would work something out with the lawyer on fees.

In turn, the lawyer called and left a message that he would take $5,000 to show up at court. He reminded the client that she could get a mortgage on her house. The client, having been instructed by the compassionate lawyer to put things in writing, emailed and said she did not have the $5,000, but asked if a trial preparation meeting on Sunday was still scheduled. She never got a response.

On Monday, the lawyer showed up two minutes before the start of trial. Before they went into the courtroom, the lawyer handed the client a document, telling her to sign it. The client resisted but kept the document to later learn that the lawyer was attempting to put a lien on the client's business.

The client was not prepared, the witnesses had not been spoken to, and the client was withholding visitation of her son for no real good reason as she walked into the courtroom.

Over the lunch break of the first day of trial, the lawyer again said he was going to withdraw. At the end of the first day, the lawyer walked out of the courtroom without talking to the client. The next day, during the questioning of the client by her own lawyer, the lawyer asked a lot of questions about the client's assets, almost like the tone of a judgment debtor examination. The issue of withholding visitation also came up. It turns out the client had been served with a contempt for withholding through her counsel, but she had never been informed by the lawyer.

The client ultimately unraveled on the stand, telling the judge through tears she withheld visitation on the advice of her lawyer, and that the lawyer tried to extort fees from her, even up to the time they walked into the courtroom. The furious judge put the lawyer on the stand, swore him in, and asked him about some of the events.

The judge ended up fining the lawyer $4,500, including $500 for each of nine missed visits after he admitted he advised withholding the child. Even though the judge was furious because of the situation over attorney's fees, he was powerless to order fees to be refunded in the proceeding. The client is now seeking a refund through the fee arbitration committee. She spent all that money and virtually nothing happened to change her situation.

When I met with her to hear her story, I was sad to see the level of shame the woman client felt. She told me that she felt badly that she picked the wrong lawyer in the first place. I assured her she did nothing wrong and she had every reason to believe the lawyer would help her and that she was harmed by a lawyer through no fault of her own. We had a further conversation about forgiving herself. She hugged me as she left the office and said she felt better.

Total cost

What a case will cost a client in total can be a difficult area to discuss. Sometimes it is difficult to tell, but it's important to give a client some insight into what it will cost them in total. Clients deserve to know a range of the total amount they can expect to pay. They also need to be told, in detail, the efforts that cost money and the efforts that don't.

For example, explaining legal discovery to clients is essential. They don't know what it is and how costly it can run. Even saying the word "deposition" in passing to a client is not enough. Clients need to have each segment of effort explained to them so when they ask, or even sometimes demand to undertake costly depositions or discovery, they can understand how costs go up exponentially.

A client came into my office recently seeking to switch lawyers. She handed me a folder of interrogatories, a request for production of documents, and other legal discovery documents, and then asked me why her lawyer had sent it. "Shouldn't I have had a say in whether this went out?" she asked. Based on what I saw in the file, some of it was necessary, but most of it was not. Compassionate lawyers keep clients involved every step of the way.

Using fees as leverage to "win"

The idea of using legal fees as leverage is "fair game" in the legal world. Costs of defense are often part of the negotiation dialogue in personal injury cases. To "bury them in legal discovery" is a battle cry in cases where deep-pocketed clients use their lawyers to burden the other side, leaving them no choice but to surrender.

This mentality is particularly troubling in the family law arena. One party, in many instances the mother, surrenders some arrangement on custody or child support not only because she runs out of money, but because she is emotionally worn out. Knowing that this "egg shell" party is vulnerable, the other lawyer uses excessive legal maneuvers as a strategy. Going to court to ask for interim fees may keep the fight alive, but in the end the higher income spouse prevails on the endurance meter. Who suffers or reaps the effects of such efforts? The children.

A lawyer might throw interrogatories, requests for production of documents, and requests for admissions at the opposing party in an effort to intimidate, even when such efforts are "overkill." The receiving client gets agitated and wants to know why his or her lawyer isn't doing the same thing back. Lawyers should talk in detail with their clients about the need and the consequences of doing retaliatory discovery, including the cost of doing so.

Regrettably I often have to tell clients that a lot of the cost depends on the lawyer the other side hires. This is a delicate subject when trying to respect my colleagues, but I must be honest with the client. I let them know that if a lawyer sends me an inordinate amount of legal discovery I have to take the time to answer and produce documents in compliance with the rules, often also enlisting the help of support staff. When clients have to fill out legal discovery, they inquire as to why we are not doing the same. In initial consults, I tell clients that if the other lawyer sends it, we have to incur costs to respond, but we will thoughtfully decide if we need to send out the same to the other side before we just do it as a retaliation.

I recently went to a training for "streamlined protocols" for a collaborative divorce. The instructors developed a format by which the parties can obtain a collaborative divorce in a cost conscious, yet thorough way. As we were taught the streamlined protocols, the other lawyers asked about "add ons" that clients often request because of their heightened emotional state.

The group suggested telling clients that the streamlined protocols are the basic necessities for the divorce and additional matters or events are treated like a "change order." Most people understand that if they have a contractor bid a job and then they want changes, change orders cost money. Lawyers can help the clients evaluate the effectiveness of the efforts recommended by the client or requested by the client once he or she has undertaken the work, and can let the client know that the change orders cost money from the original budget. Either way, clients deserve to be kept abreast of what is going on and what efforts can come up in a case that were unexpected. They have a voice in the change orders.

Billing review firms

I was saddened to learn that "lawyer bill review companies" have sprung up across the country. Large consumers of legal services, usually large businesses, hire these companies to review bills and identify controversial areas for negotiation and reduction in fees. In searching the Internet I found a bill review company called "The Devil's Advocate."

Before I was in-house counsel at Rodeway Inns, Inc. over thirty years ago, all of the legal work was done by outside counsel. The human resource director reviewed the legal bills and determined whether the charges were fair. However, as a nonlawyer, she had no standard to know how to actually read the bill.

Eventually I asked to take over the bill review. I found many areas where the outside law firm could be more efficient. They weren't doing anything wrong or unethical, but there was a lot of duplicative and nonessential work. I would venture that most clients are scared to challenge a lawyer on the fees that appear on their bills. Because clients are intimidated, lawyers can bill freely with little consequence. The skeptics call this a "license to steal." Compassionate lawyers are judicious in their billing and would withstand any type of audit from other lawyers or clients.

As a result of some lawyer's billing practices, insurance companies regulate the fees their defense counsel charge on legal matters. One might argue that it is reasonable to keep lawyers' billing in line, but like regulated medicine, is it reasonable to have the professional restricted in using his or her best judgment?

Recovering attorney's fees

Recovery of attorney's fees is always a question raised by clients. When clients hire a lawyer, they willingly and mindlessly spend money on legal efforts. However, the client may be in a trance of emotion that ultimately catches up. After some time the client may wake up to see the legal bill is a runaway train, and then hope the lawyer can force the other party to pay the bill.

Statutes and caselaw often make it difficult for clients to recover legal fees, as they limit the ability to collect from the other party. The other party may have also endured financial hardship due to their own legal fees or to extra medical bills, lost jobs, inability to be productive, etc.

Our clients often don't understand a judgment for fees doesn't just come, as one often has to pay a lawyer to collect them through an entirely separate procedure. Often times, after the case has settled, everyone is furious over cost so they go to court only on the issue of legal fees. The trial only ends up costing more money. I have yet to hear of a client that is content with the way the court typically rules on legal fees.

Expert witnesses

Some cases also require experts to participate. Business evaluators, subject matter experts, scientists, accountants, doctors, and forensic experts may be needed. Clients don't often expect additional charges for these people. If a case might involve an expert the compassionate lawyer will inform the client of the possibility and provide ample information on fees.

Some lawyers have their cadre of experts that they bring in on many or most cases. Over the years I have seen experts whom were not critical to the outcome of the case, but were brought in to work on the case. Usually one side hires an expert, then the other side hires another to contradict and have dueling opinions.

The advent of collaborative law has been a wonderful way to curb expert fees. While it started in the family law arena, it has now spread to civil cases of all types. In the collaborative setting, the parties agree they will hire an expert for "the collective", not working for one party or the other. A true expert who is qualified and impartial can craft an expert opinion that is fair. If the lawyers are suspicious of experts and their allegiance, they can each identify an expert and the two experts pick a third who is the final expert for the collective.

Public response

The public's response to these billing issues has been two-fold. Legal zoom.com and other self help methods have sprung up. Clients can access legal kiosks or online systems in some larger cities. People are making their own deals to avoid lawyers and as a result some deals are inadequate, unfair, incomplete, potentially illegal, or unenforceable. We rely on court administration or judges to screen these out, but how fair and reasonable is that given their large caseloads and budget cuts? People walk away from their legal matter often not seeing or knowing how their resolution will play out over the long run.

In some jurisdictions "document preparers" have sprung up. In some cities, non-lawyer mediators hang around the courthouse to help people resolve conflict. The lawyers and the bar association, understandably take on some of these individuals for the unauthorized practice of law.

But where are the moderately priced, more accessible lawyers? It seems there is either the "mainstream" lawyer, including the high priced barracudas, or the pro bono lawyers, but not much in between.

Legal insurance is another way of handling this. Referred to as "prepaid legal services" this insurance is often offered as a benefit to company employees. Insurance companies recruit lawyers to offer their legal services at a discounted rate. The problem is that many of these policies allow you a reduced hourly rate, but don't regulate how many hours a lawyer can charge. Therefore, clients expecting substantial savings may be disappointed even in light of the perceived discounts.

Because a large part of my practice is mediating, clients will often call wanting to hire a mediator because "we don't want to pay lawyers." They are often surprised to hear that I am a lawyer in addition to being a mediator, but they categorize me as "different than them" because I am perceived as a problem-solver. It makes me sad to hear that people are trying to avoid dealing with lawyers.

Lawyers and money

As with all other aspects of compassionate lawyering, the "self-care" components also apply to having a healthy relationship with money. My experience in both living with and among lawyers, as well as mediating for them in their personal lives, is that we don't often have the best money management skills.

When lawyers have to live from contingent fee recovery to contingent fee recovery, it can be difficult to budget and create a cash flow. Also, many self-employed lawyers have to pay estimated tax payments and may have difficulty doing appropriate tax planning. Earning a lot of money, and managing it well are not always hand-in- hand.

I am unaware of many law schools that teach specifics about money management. Law students may leave law school with extensive student debt. If they cannot find a job upon graduation, it can be tempting to charge a higher rate or to engage in controversial billing practices.

My daughter received her master's degree in education. She informed me that if she teaches certain subjects for a period of time in certain jurisdictions, she receives loan forgiveness. Why don't we do this with law students? Why don't we forgive student loan debt for those that work in inner-city legal aid offices, provide pro bono work, or set up legal consultation clinics in underserved neighborhoods? Or for those who use their incredible legal skills in creative ways we can't even imagine?

Even for more seasoned lawyers, understanding money in general isn't a life skill that automatically comes with a license to practice law. Misuse of finances is often an obstacle to finishing well. If we aren't equipping lawyers to properly manage money and prepare for their future, they may be tempted to continue to work long past their shelf life. This not only runs a risk of lawyers working past their effectiveness, but they occupy positions that could be filled with younger lawyers looking to begin their careers.

Something I have done with young lawyers who worked for me over the years is to give them a consultation with a certified financial planner. The consultation equips them to understand their relationship with money and hopefully wakes them up to the fact they need to manage it wisely.

Money management is a spiritual journey

Lawyers are often high profile in the community, meaning they have a "persona" to uphold. They may fall prey to trinkets and trappings of wealth that, at the end of the day, they really can't afford. Sometimes money starts to flow in and the lawyer is not able to handle it. They may spoil their family into living a life of largesse so that the family members have a warped sense of money entitlement and the lawyer continues to work to support such a lifestyle. Sometimes lawyers may give gifts and other luxuries to their families in lieu of spending time with them because the job is so demanding, diminishing time spent with family members.

Unfortunately, the luxury of making a good sum of money then indulging yourself and others creates a number of harmful by-products. The worst of these is the idea of "golden handcuffs." That is, you must stay in the practice of law even if it does not suit you, because you get used to the lifestyle and you don't want to give it up.

By living within or even beneath your means, a lawyer can have ultimate freedom. Saving money, resisting debt, and having vigilance about spending can create a character that endures. It also models for those around you how to do to the same.

Many lawyers I know don't have a will or an estate plan. One lawyer said he didn't need a will because he put everything for his partner into joint tenancy. Most probate lawyers advise that you still need a will, and perhaps a living will. Failing to set up strong financial planning is risky for the lawyer and also hurtful to the family.

Where does a healthy relationship with money fit into the compassionate lawyer's life? Is this something that needs attention?

Our profession turned a corner along the way, away from healing and more toward big business. The ability to charge big dollars for our services surely had an impact on our path. In our society, people who are highly educated and charge a lot of money for their work gain power, and power, if we are not careful, corrupts. How we spend the money we make shines a light to others who we inspire. Could the money aspects of the law be part of where we got off track?

Chapter 11

Future

**Compassionate lawyers work to create change and innovation
in the legal profession for the common good**

Lawyers, do we make the world a better place because of our lawyering?
What are we leaving as our legacy to the lawyers to come? Will they
practice law as we have done, or differently? As I look into the future
of our profession, I envision many changes.

Law school

In 2013, President Obama gave a presentation at Binghamton University in New York and said he believed law school should be two years
long, rather than three.[1] He elaborated that law students should use
their final two semesters to gain work experience by clerking in a firm
at a reduced rate. His comments were directed at methods of keeping
costs down for students getting out of law school.

When I went to law school, there was the common saying, "In the first
year they scare you to death; in the second year they work you to death;
and in the third year they bore you to death." Whether law schools set
out to do that or students automatically react in that manner, it proves
to be true for many. Are three years necessary? First, let's examine the
way students are taught.

Learning to think like a lawyer

Part of the indoctrination into fear for law students is the use of the Socratic method in the classroom. In this model the law professor poses questions to the group, in an attempt to stimulate critical thinking. Law students are put on the spot and expected to answer intelligently under pressure in front of their peers. In some instances, aggressive professors can "grill" a student for large blocks of time, again, in front of their peers.

One study has shown that the use of this method, "can leave even strong students with a baseline sense of incompetence if emphasized to the exclusion of the many other skills that students know will be necessary for law practice."[2] I was clueless from day one on how to engage in the Socratic method. I shuddered and tried to minimize my physical body, to be avoid being called on by the professors. Operating in high anxiety does not make for a desirable learning environment.

Another study conducted by Elizabeth Mertz, an anthropologist, law professor and Senior Fellow at the American Bar Foundation looked at students in a first year contracts class at eight different law schools.[3] She found that in all of the classes students were taught to think like lawyers by discounting their own moral values, setting aside their own feelings of empathy and compassion, and substituting a strictly analytical and strategic mode of thinking.[4] Based upon her observations, Mertz concludes that law school has the goal of changing people's values and encouraging students to unmoor themselves from moral reasoning.[5] The result of this approach, according to Mertz, is that "students lose their sense of self and become analytically and emotionally detatched."[6]

I truly learned to be a lawyer under my Dad's tutelage. I sat in on depositions, client meetings, trials, hearings, and even worked with the firm bookkeeper on financial issues. If I hadn't had his law office to work in, I would have felt ill-prepared to practice despite the excellent theoretical training I got in law school. Gratefully, there are more clinical programs available in law schools now.

Law schools of the future

Now imagine future law school education involving the following:

The law school has quality and engaged professors: professors who are interested in mentoring and engaging with students as much as they are interested in scholarly endeavors and tenure. The younger professors are fresh off of practice in their respective fields. The mid-career and seasoned veterans have had accountability partners and mentors throughout their teaching careers and have avoided blowout, burnout, and/or plateauing. Any professors that have burned out or plateaued have been removed.

Each law school professor has taken a two-day coaching training with intermittent refreshers or advanced courses, and has also attended seminars on compassionate lawyering topics. On the first day of law school, each professor meets with their pool of advisees, introducing themselves and each other. Appointments are set for group sessions monthly between the professor and his/her advisees. Individual appointments are also made so that each student can express to their assigned professor their goals and desires for their law school experience. Individual accountability goals are established and weekly follow up emails may be agreed upon.

The career services office has identified alumni and community lawyers who desire to mentor a law student and who have also been trained in coaching and compassionate lawyer skills. Law students are matched with a community lawyer whom they meet with monthly. If schedules get busy, meetings may be held via Skype or Facetime if necessary. The mentoring lawyer invites the law student to come to the firm or in-house legal department and "shadow" his or her work. The lawyers introduce the law student to each member of their firm or team, or other lawyers in the student's field of interest. Law students go to the courthouse and attend a meeting with judges, who welcome them to the law. Judges also invite and encourage students to sit in on trials.

Law school courses are exciting and engaging. The Socratic method takes a back seat to innovative learning styles. Technology is utilized. Practicing attorneys and real clients come into the classroom to share stories and answer questions. Many of the classes are practical and clinical in nature. Students learn, in their very first year, how to interview a client and those recruited to "play" the client give direct feedback. The students are video recorded in many of their efforts and then they debrief with the client and professor.

The law school has healthy foods available. Junk food and soda pop are nowhere to be found in vending machines. Coffee is freshly perked. There is a salad bar, a juice bar, and a workout room as well as a silent lounge. When I went to law school, the beloved "quiet lounge" was a haven for stressed out law students. However, the room recently got remodeled into open-air seating. While the new layout is gorgeous, every law school needs a quiet room.

There are on-site resources for students struggling with depression and other mental health challenges. Students are taught about the dangers of mind, body, spirit negligence to self and given empowering information on healthy lifestyles. Lawyers who have dealt with addiction will lecture at the law school about the dangers of stressors of the practice.

If law school remains three years in duration, the coursework must be exhilarating and vibrant. The academic advisor and mentor lawyer have both had a strong accountability relationship with the law student, helping him or her navigate through classes and challenges. Students have a solid grounding in their mind, body, spirit wholeness. Students have been exposed to "the real world" throughout law school. They have also taken coursework in such topics as starting well, purpose, empathy, and trustworthiness.

In the third year, students are obligated to take on coursework in a practical setting. They have the opportunity to work as a clerk at a firm, in-house legal department or in a Legal Aid setting. They may choose to set up their own firm or solo practice. When I clerked for my

Dad, as a law student, none of my professors knew what I was doing in my spare time so they never asked if I was learning anything. In the future, the third year professor specialists will assist the students in their practical endeavors.

Students that work in their third year are paid a reasonable wage. They report to their supervising professor to dissect what they are learning and whether that particular job or area of law is a good fit. The student and professor identify additional efforts the student may undertake to supplement his or her learning curve. When this is the case, both the firm and the student win. The firm has an engaged law student with an educational support system and they don't have to invest time in training. The student makes money and gets an introduction to the lawyer world, testing the market to find an area of law that feeds their passion. This is foundational in making sure law students are equipped to "hit the ground running" upon graduation.

As I write this book, there are economic struggles going on for lawyers. The market is tight for jobs and students are setting up their own law offices although many are ill-equipped to do so. What if, in the third year of law school, the law school staff and faculty was the support team for students going on to be solo or small practice lawyers?

In essence, under this format the law school faculty is like a senior partner/office administrator/tax advisor all in one. They can assist the student with law office management assistance, help them set up an LLC if they choose, identify appropriate technology and software, coach in client intake methods, help in trust account management, and also confer on legal issues as they come up. They might even sit in on a consult with the student and debrief afterwards, or sit in at a hearing to watch the student and debrief afterwards.

Those that work in Legal Aid will likely gain the most experience. At my law school, there is a legal clinic where indigent clients can rely on law students, under the supervision of a professor, to assist them with a wide array of legal matters, including family law, criminal defense, transactional, juvenile and elder law. Students are in the courtroom and handle cases with practicing attorneys on the other side. However, the list of students waiting to get into the clinic is a long one.

Furthermore, law students will receive course grades but there will be no class ranking, which only discourages cooperation and pits everyone against everyone else. Even law schools will not have ranking, the current ranking system being a matter of controversy. In a recent study about what makes a lawyer happy, the results confirmed an "almost meaningless correlation between lawyer well-being and graduating from a higher-tier law school."[7] Further, both depression and positive affect were unrelated to school ranking. Yet law schools and employers look to grades and rankings, and the ranking of the law school.

There may be a law review but in all honesty, when was the last time anyone really read a law review article? I would venture that if you take a look at the titles of notes and articles in law reviews, most of them sound incredibly boring or irrelevant. Since most law reviews only accept students in the top 10% of the class, the other 90% sit on the sidelines.

In addition to law review, what about a law school magazine? Students can write both scholarly and practical articles that can be sent out on Twitter, Facebook, or other social media, to educate the public. Why aren't more students being published in the monthly state bar association magazines? Why isn't there a law school blog?

Large amounts of student loan debt is also problematic for up and coming lawyers. Dealing with money management in general is an important topic. Money management will become a required course in law school in the future and each student would meet with a certified financial planner or similarly qualified financial advisor as part of their curriculum. Those people would be on staff, even if only as an adjunct.

Students would have structured budgets, a healthy understanding of money, earning and spending goals, a five year plan for their financial lives, a sensitivity to credit card spending and borrowing, and a strategy for loan repayment. They may even enhance their personal credit scores if they need some "clean up" in the money department. As they launch into the law practice, they will be more conversant in money issues than 99% of the general public, which is what they should be as leaders in society.

These innovations require a whole new paradigm for law schools. Currently overstaffed with scholarly endeavors, the professors of the future will include those who understand technology and the business side of law. Professors will be mentors, encouragers, and supporters, eliminating the style of intimidation and humiliation that still has a remnant in some areas of legal education. Students that desire to be professors will be inspired by the fact that a broad array of skills such as coaching, mentoring, and supporting will become important for selection, rather than the narrow one dimensional focus.

Bar exam

There is controversy swirling, in many states, regarding the bar exam. Is it a necessary and/or helpful threshold measurement of law students, to determine whether they should be in the profession?

I am not a fan of exams in general, but the bar exam is more than just a test. In most states it also includes an extensive background check and other checkpoints into an individual's character and criminal record.

I believe lawyers should have impeccable credentials along with character and integrity, not just legal education. As previously mentioned, leaders often finish poorly because they are not held to specific accountability. If we have people entering the profession with deficiencies, putting them in power and in touch with the wounded, we are asking for trouble.

As for the bar exam itself, I am in favor of retaining it. However, it should be broader based. I will never forget my first attempt at the bar exam when I fumbled on a real estate question. I chuckle as I think back to when I successfully passed the exam. It was so impractical.

Nobody ever told me that when I prepare a Quit Claim Deed for a client it has to be recorded at the county recorder's office. I learned that from the lawyers I worked for when I started the practice of law. So, how helpful is an exam that tests on a lot of theory, but doesn't provide a bit of guidance into the practical aspects of the law? Is it unthinkable to propose that as part of the bar exam you have to draft pleadings in a case? Or you have to write an essay on trust account management? Or you are given a fact scenario that requires you to e-file pleadings or a real estate deed? The bar exam simply needs to be more practically based.

Innovative ideas in the profession

As a lawyer passionate for the Integrative Law movement, I have come across new, practical concepts. I have actually located some of the lawyers championing these causes and contacted them via Skype, email and telephone to discuss their concepts directly. Hearing about these innovative measures excites me.

I am amazed at the number of lawyers who are holding tightly to the traditional practice of law and who view the innovative methods as threats to the sanctity of the profession. Here are just a few initiatives that have sprung up from compassionate lawyers:

Conscious contracting

Lawyers are used to drafting contracts with litanies of protections and exchanging them back and forth until both parties are satisfied. Conscious contracting, on the other hand, begins with thorough discussion with both parties together as the parties come to an agreement on their shared vision, mission, and values, as well as their promises and even their future fears. Then, the contract is drafted to provide conflict mechanisms that revolve around the agreement. The parties constantly review the elements of the contract, especially if conflict arises or there is a change in circumstances. The contract can always be altered.

Linda Alvarez, a California lawyer who is proactive in the movement, explains that "Rather than using their contract as a weapons cache stockpiled in case of dispute, the parties can write a document that serves as a guide and support to their own, intentional system and structure within, and with the support of the greater, conventional frame and framework."[8]

Alvarez also signs an engagement conscious contract with her own clients, which states: "[My] mission is to support clients in conducting their legal affairs in alignment with their values, their principles and their vision for a better world, and to stimulate and sustain positive relationships and enterprises, with positive results and proceeds – for [my] clients, for the local and global communities, and for future generations."[9]

Lawyers involved in the conscious contracting movement report satisfied clients in transactional, family, and business association matters. By having a discussion and developing a relationship before contracting, the lawyer acts as a preventative conflict manager, helping resolve issues before they create high conflict.

Personally, I see many situations where conscious contracting is useful. For example, a lawyer I know drafted a prenuptial agreement for his client, a man who was getting married. The woman fiancée being asked to sign it came to me to review and explain the prenuptial. It wasn't long before the tightly worded prenuptial caused her to cry, as it restricted her from any recourse in the event of divorce and called for her to waive her spousal statutory rights in the event of death. The man had a family business that he wanted to protect. The woman was quitting her productive job in sales and marketing to help raise the man's children from a former marriage and have the ability to entertain his clients. She told me, "A man who would put this in front of me is not the man I thought I was marrying." I advised the woman to discuss the situation with her fiancée.

It seemed that the man's lawyer simply filled out a "standard form prenuptial" and sent it to the wife with no detailed conversation about its purpose. The next day, the man sent both lawyers a very stern email stating that the prenup was not at all what he wanted and instead he simply intended to protect the business for his children. Over the next few days, we emailed back and forth discussing various financial safeguards for his wife-to-be. My client was relieved we had reviewed the document closely together. I couldn't help but wonder how the lawyer's standard form and cavalier attitude put a rift in the relationship, at least until it got cleared up. I wondered how a joint meeting and conscious contract would have been a better fit.

Imagine the impact of lawyers engaged in conscious contracting with clients that needed a contract or similar document drafted. If everyone's values and missions were aligned in the first place, one must wonder whether compassionate lawyers could proactively help save marriages as well as business, employment, and other familial relationships.

Collaborative law

Collaborative law is another process that has given us an environment to respect and honor our clients. This style of lawyering was developed by University of Iowa Law School graduate Stu Webb, who wrote a letter to a Justice of the Supreme Court of his home state of Minnesota on Valentine's Day in 1990. His letter was written to the justice after Stu had met him at a cocktail party several years prior. He had also heard the justice talk about alternative dispute a few months prior to writing the letter.

Stu had been practicing as a mediator and was struck with the observation that in some cases there was a serendipitously created "climate of positive energy" where everyone "contributed to a final settlement that satisfied all concerned" and "everyone left the conference feeling high energy, good feelings and satisfaction." His query to the justice was why lawyers couldn't create such a settlement climate deliberately through a "coterie of lawyers who would agree to take cases on a case-by-case basis for settlement only." Thus collaborative law began.

Having met Stu and been trained by him and his colleague Ron Ousky, I am not only impressed with his brilliance, I am also impressed by his courage. In 1990, mediation was fairly new. Everyone was buzzing about the process. Yet Stu, even in those early days, saw something more in the process. He took it to the next level, and then put his "crazy idea" in front of a Minnesota Supreme Court justice he had met at a cocktail party.

Most clients shun the idea of going to court, usually because they feel they lose control of their destiny by turning over the power to complete strangers. In a collaborative case, the parties and the lawyers are all in the same room for the bulk of the legal work. The parties sign an agreement that they will not go to court. However, if they conclude negotiations have broken down and they need to seek judicial intervention, they must dismiss the collaborative lawyers at the table and hire two new lawyers.

The parties further agree to voluntarily exchange all documents without the need for formal discovery. Discovery is costly and a billable time exericse, so this voluntary exchange is beneficial for both parties. If it happens that we need an expert for financial input, the parties hire one for the collective who looks to the future on behalf of both clients. The collaborative lawyers don't resort to "their" expert to wrestle with the other lawyer's expert causing duplicative charges and more stress to the parties.

Some question the lawyer's ethical advocacy in a collaborative matter. However, when I represent a client at a four-way meeting, I will not hesitate to give my legal advice to my client. Although it may be in front of the other party, I am still advocating for my client. I am still mindful and craft my words carefully, so as not to disrepect the other lawyer or party's perspective. I may also point out options that help the other party if they do not adversely impact my own client.

Further, when lawyers in a collaborative case disagree in any way, we do so respectfully. When we respectfully engage and negotiate in front of clients, we demonstrate how people on conflicting sides can resolve differences out of compassion and highly calibrated emotions. When clients see this, they themselves seem to negotiate more calmly and with dignity. There is no behind the scenes between the parties of "my lawyer said that!" or "you are lying, my lawyer told me differently."

Collaborative law began in family law, but has continued to grow. It is now used in probate/trust and estate contests, healthcare conflicts, employment disputes and construction claims, among others.

The most magical thing that happens is that both clients often end up liking both lawyers. My colleague and I recently did a collaborative divorce on a very long-term marriage and at the conclusion my client hugged the other lawyer!

Peacemaking circles

Based on the tradition of indigenous people to sit around the campfire in circles, and families to gather at the kitchen table in a circle, lawyers are working with problems using the circle model. The model is most widely used in restorative justice, involving victims and perpetrators of crimes sitting in circle with others involved in the system that interfaces with criminal matters.

One hallmark of the circle process involves each participant speaking, but only when they have been passed, and are holding, a talking piece. The talking piece is passed around the group and each person may "pass" or may engage in addressing the question posed by the facilitator. The dialogue is woven by storytelling, where participants share their lives in a safe and calm environment.

In our ancestors' societies nobody was thrown away. Anyone who was acting in dissonance with the community was seen to have been let down by the community. Now our model is that we throw away, lock up, send away or execute those that let down the community. Instead of finding ways to support and create a haven for repentance and remorse, we shame and magnify differences.

The circle process has been successfully used in schools, neighborhoods, workplaces, religious institutions and social agencies. "The under-lying philosophy of Circles acknowledges that we are all in need of help and that helping others helps us at the same time," writes Kay Pranis in *"The Little Book of Circles."*[10]

The participants of the Circle benefit from the collective wisdom of everyone in the Circle. Participants are not divided into givers and receivers: everyone is both a giver and receiver. Circles draw on the life experience and wisdom of all participants to generate new understandings of the problem and new possibilities for solutions."[11]

Specially trained lawyers are great facilitators of circles. Imagine the diverse problem solving and conflict resolution that can be facilitated in the circle process. Having had the privilege of training in Circles from Kay Pranis, I saw first-hand how compassionate lawyers can use the process in many different ways.

Law offices

I have had the pleasure of working in medium sized firms, small firms, corporate in-house, and solo practice. I've seen law offices that look like museums and I've practiced in a remodeled house that felt like home. I've also traveled to other law offices to take depositions and conduct mediations.

As I look into the future, I dream of a type of law office where clients come to begin healing their lives. Because mediation and collaborative law are my passion, my ideal law office would be a place that doesn't resemble an office at all.

I envision a quiet setting in a lush natural environment and a building that resembles a modern cabin. Clients are greeted warmly and feel at home in a cozy and comfortable space. I think of President Jimmy Carter's middle east peace talks that took place at Camp David in 1978. President Clinton also held peace talks there in 2000. Presidents often go there for retreat and host foreign dignitaries.

Pictures of Camp David show a wooded retreat, outside the bustle of Washington, D.C.. Photographs of the meetings held there show both a casual environment with couches and large chairs and rooms that have a meeting table. Outside there are trails to walk among the trees in solitude.

I can think of nothing better than to use such a facility for collaborative problem solving and mediation. Instead of shuttling back and forth between two stark conference rooms I dream of walking outside on a beautiful day with a party in conflict to discuss their positions and interests in privacy.

Until that time comes, our offices should reflect compassion, as well as peaceful and calm resolution. Instead of stark quarters and secretaries answering buzzing phones, there will be a more intimate setting where clients are greeted warmly, rather than someone sitting behind a desk asking, "Can I help you?"

Inner offices, where the client meets with the lawyer, will have comfortable chairs and the lawyer can sit side-by-side with the client. If the client and lawyer meet in a conference room, a round table in a smaller room works better than a large conference table in a big room. Gone will be the "corner offices" of big-named partners. Spaces will be smaller and warmer.

Some lawyers are beginning this process in revolutionary ways. Houston Attorney Kristin Scheel at one time housed her office in a space that doubled as a yoga studio. Her philosophy was that yoga and her style of law practice were based on the same principals. Schell defines this principle, "If you have too much ease and softness, that would reduce the impact. And too much effort could cause overexertion."

Boutique firms

As I visualize the future of law firms, I envision smaller boutique firms. What I learned from my compassionate lawyer-father in his unique practice was that people came to the lawyer for any problem, even if it wasn't a legal problem. If it was a worry or concern, they knew the lawyer with the power brain and connections would help them solve their problems. The lawyer is first thought of as a problem solver.

My Dad practiced in a cozy remodeled house. I see more of those types of offices. I also see small office buildings with suites, warmly decorated and inviting. In the main suite is the "lawyer hub" with lawyers who have expertise in complimentary fields.

For example, in one building there is a family law boutique. There are family law attorneys, bankruptcy attorneys, real estate attorneys, probate attorneys and juvenile law attorneys. Perhaps there are two to three of each specialty. Clients who have questions, concerns, or problems concerning their families come to the suite and meet with the practitioners who can help them.

One attorney greets the client and does an intake while engaging in the compassionate lawyer "caring" standards. As the lawyer assesses the needs of the client, he or she might walk the client to the office of the lawyer that can best serve them, and then sit with the client as they help convey the information to the new lawyer.

What if the problem isn't a legal problem? Elsewhere in the suite, or on another floor of the small building, there are other "hubs." A financial legal hub would be headed by a tax attorney with CPA's, Certified Financial Planners, credit repair staff, mortgage brokers and other financial specialists also in the suite. The tax attorney would be the liaison for the financial problem solving and would enlist the help of the other professionals.

Another suite might involve mental health professionals including counselors, psychologists, custody evaluators, and marriage counselors. The family "triage" lawyer would be the liaison with this suite.

Why not dream big? Why not have medical practitioners, nurse practitioners, massage therapists, chiropractors, acupuncturists and physical therapists in another suite? Certainly in a personal injury focused legal hub these individuals would be invaluable.

Think of additional specialties and what companion professions might be in the suite. For employment law, add a vocational rehabilitation specialist, a headhunter, a business coach, an SBA office, a banker.

In each of these venues, law students would be working side-by-side with their attorney mentors. The lawyer has assessed the client's problems and directed him or her within the building, whenever possible, to specialists who have the skills to help the client.

In each of these office buildings there would be a gym, a meditation room or quiet lounge, a meeting room for exciting seminars, and a healthy cafeteria. The professionals, all with compassionate approaches, would need to take care of themselves. This concept is not unheard of. Companies like Apple, Google and Facebook have these facilities (lap pool, bicycle repair shops, mobile haircuts).

Granted these types of amenities cost money. But what if there were legal office parks where there was a common facility for these "mind body spirit" accommodations?

Corporate legal departments

What about legal departments in big companies? My own hometown of Des Moines, Iowa, is the third largest venue for insurance companies in the world, just behind London, England and Hartford, Connecticut. Why not implement some of these future ideas for lawyers in those positions? What about in-house lawyers or lawyer mediators who could help problem solve employee issues in these big insurance companies? Would having problem-solving lawyers in the building help employee morale?

What are the working environments for in-house attorneys in big corporations? Many lawyers I know in this type of environment work in cubicles and meet in conference rooms. All that brain power is condensed in the "legal department." Would it be of value to put these brilliant compassionate problem solvers throughout the company to interface with the other departments? This is just a brainstorming thought. The lawyer is usually the "go to" person or the point guard for problem solving in many of these corporate environments.

Fees

How do future attorney's fees come into play? Would lawyers make less money? It depends. At the end of the day, the value of a lawyer's problem solving is tremendous. I am not suggesting lawyers don't get paid for their work, or that they get paid less. Rather, I am suggesting that customer service oriented subjects such as when the client signs the fee agreement, how the initial consultation is billed, and other financial considerations, are worked out and communicated clearly.

The billing format would be something quite different from the archaic billable hour. Fees would be custom designed depending on what the client needs and fees will be clearly explained. Fee agreements will be conscious contracts, identifying the work to be done and the goals to be handled. Lawyers will check in with clients after the matter formally closes to see how the client is doing and to provide accountability for the action items that resulted from the representation.

Can you see a world where the first stop with any problem was to a lawyer? And thereafter the lawyer was a lifelong resource for clients, as they experience other types of conflict?

Courthouses

I was raised in a generation of lawyers that have had the privilege to go to court in some of the most beautiful, historic buildings in the country. These majestic castles house history, musty law books, ancient records, and busy personnel.

Going to the courthouse as a young lawyer was one of the most exciting things I did in the practice. Trying a case before a judge sitting on the bench in a black robe, exuding wisdom, and brilliance in the law is the pinnacle of any lawyer's career.

Unfortunately, or fortunately, depending on your perspective, these types of forums are no longer useful or practical. Only about 3% of cases actually go to trial. Most record keeping is electronic, creating a reduced need for space to store documents. The law libraries are all online and not in thick, heavy legal books with pocket parts. Fewer cases go to court, so the grandiose courtrooms often sit idle. Self-help kiosks dot the hallways and administrative offices within some courthouses. Courthouses are operating at deficits, requiring a reduction in services and streamlined operating hours.

In the future I believe there will still be courthouses. However, they will be smaller and run much more efficiently. I have less of a vision or hunch on what they might be physically, but I do see the compassionate lawyers inside of them. Ken Ricci of the American Institute of Architects (AIA) suggests that the new courthouses give ample space for settlement activities.[12] Each settlement zone will be under the control of a judge's staff but accessible to attorneys.[13] "These spaces will have daylight and views to the outside that promote normative behavior, reduce tensions and elevate the spirit. These spaces also will have modern technology, alcoves for informal one-on-one conversations that promote negotiations, more spaces for group meetings, and work areas for outside counsel. Judges will still have chambers, nearby and private, together with their clerks and support staff."[14]

Trial lawyers are some of the most skilled and brilliant people on the planet. While I have tried many cases and advocated in many hearings, I don't fancy myself a trial lawyer. After a few days in trial, my preparation and efforts often took so much out of me I would have to go to bed and sleep for hours to recover from the physical and emotional exertion. Yet I could mediate for 12 hours straight and still feel energized at the conclusion of the case. Each of us is "wired differently" as a lawyer.

In the future, those who are called to be trial lawyers will be compassionate trial lawyers. They will work closely with their clients to prepare them for trial, to explain what they are doing to represent the client, and to constantly keep the client informed as to what is going on during the trial.

Best of all, these gladiators will display the utmost in professionalism. They will be totally prepared, arriving early to court with their case ready to present. They will have mastered the finest uses of technology to make the trial a high class presentation. They won't take a case to trial because it is "good money" and show up with a halfhearted presentation and preparation.

Cases will be tried in courtrooms with flexible and adaptable administrators. Lawyers will have the ability to utilize technology so jurors and clients alike can understand the case in a manner that is clear, understandable, and visual.

The most exciting thing I see in my mind's eye are the jurists who sit at the helm in these courthouses. Compassionate lawyers will be selected as judges based on merit and skill, not as payback for political favors. Judges are those who have been trial lawyers and were amongst the finest in their lawyer lives. Judges will be those who know the law, love the law, and are alert and attentive to the case and the trial. Judges will be those who make their decisions based on the law and their wisdom, and are immune from other influences.

The multi-door courthouse

Developed by Harvard Law Professor Frank E.A. Sander, the multi-door courthouse directs court cases to the most appropriate methods of dispute resolution, saving time and money for both the courts and the participants or litigants.[15] Cases are routed to mediation, arbitration, early neutral evaluation or mini trials.

Sander was teaching family law at Harvard and had participated in some labor arbitrations when he noticed dissatisfaction in the way family law cases were resolved. He began to consider the efficiency and satisfaction of labor arbitrations. He wrote down some thoughts on partnering the two as alternatives to traditional resolution.

Sander's ideas caught the attention of Chief Justice Warren Burger, who asked Sander to come to Washington to speak with him about the topic and to deliver a paper at the 1976 Pound Conference.[16] Sander's creation of the "comprehensive justice center" was renamed "the multi-door courthouse" by the ABA when it did an article about the concept and depicted a number of doors on the cover.[17]

Various jurisdictions have incorporated the concept with excellent success. Now there are even "multi-door courthouse" programs in foreign countries, including Lagos, Nigeria.[18]

In addition to the innovation of the concept, what is notable is that this whole idea was the brainchild of compassionate lawyer Frank Sander, who wanted to find a better way for families to resolve disputes. It was also compassionate Supreme Court Chief Justice Warren Burger, who advocated for the concept and championed it to fruition simply by endorsing it. The reach is now worldwide. This is a perfect example of the power of compassionate lawyers to literally change the world.

Mediation centers

The multi-door courthouse could be in the actual courthouse, or it could be a justice center outside the courthouse. In the future I believe these multi door courthouses, largely mediation centers, will be the primary places citizens go to resolve problems. Compassionate lawyer mediators will be on hand to assist.

I don't believe lawyers have a lock on serving as mediators. In my own practice, I have used lawyers, businesspersons, therapists and laypersons as mediators. In my work with the State Justice Institute grant back in the 1990's, I trained mediators from all these walks of life. Every person on the planet could benefit from mediation training.

However, people's problems get more and more complicated every day. There are often legal nuances to them that require legal troubleshooting. Some cases don't settle in mediation, requiring that they go on to more traditional venues such as court. Those cases can be referred to compassionate lawyers who are in the boutique firms described above.

What I have seen happening is that lawyers are trying to force their traditional litigation paradigm into the mediation world. The lawyers may use aggressive and sometimes intimidating tactics in mediation, which is supposed to be a calm, problem-solving environment.

Even the mediation training I took 30 years ago is not the same as I teach today. My own style of mediation has evolved as well. In the "old days" we "played devils advocate" and reminded clients about the "big bad courthouse" and how they didn't want to go there. In many ways, the intimidation and fear factor was a big part of strong arming parties to settle. Tricks on numbers were a highlight of mediation training programs.

What has become clear to me after years of mediation practice, and what the future will require for mediators, is many of the same things contained in the compassionate lawyer paradigm: deep listening, empathy, and helping clients find courage to take charge of and transform their lives. Mediators must become peacemakers and problem solvers. If we can channel our lawyer power brains to facilitate discussions with the parties, we can come up with creative, comprehensive agreements that not only "settle the case," but that transform lives.

In the future, if my children encounter conflict in their lives, they are likely to say, "Let's go see the mediator," and then call to get an appointment at the mediation center. Compassionate lawyer mediators will be every bit as much an integral part of families as the family doctor, priest, or rabbi. Litigation will be a means of last resort and parties will go to the intensive courthouse only in the most extreme cases. Best of all, while driving down the street, you may see an office building sign that says "Mediation Center," just like you see Starbucks coffee shops.

Compassionate lawyer societies

How do we keep the Compassionate Lawyer movement viable? How do we prevent our profession from losing its way again? How do we distinguish to the public those who are compassionate lawyers and those who are operating under a rogue paradigm that does not serve society's highest good?

Compassionate lawyer societies must exist in every legal community. It's clear from the leadership literature that accountability is key in every successful leader. Compassionate lawyers must have community for accountability and mentoring. The societies will have meetings, and unlike the more structured Inns of Court model, the societies will be based on dialogue using the circle process described above. Compassionate lawyers will sit in circle and discuss how they can hold the value of compassion in the implementation of the seven standards. They will be in community.

Much like we have "specializing in" labels for lawyers now, what about a "seal of approval" for compassionate lawyers? Clients can identify lawyers that are labeled as compassionate lawyers because those lawyers are authorized by the state bar association to hold themselves out that way. Minimum hours of continuing legal education in compassionate lawyer topics will be required.

One of the most gratifying things I did in my legal career was go to one of the ABA's fine trial schools that lasted a full week. I walked away from that seminar invigorated by the fine instruction and the intensive experience. I was a better lawyer coming out of that school than when I went in.

I aspire to start a Compassionate Lawyer training institute. It will be like today's trial schools. Attendees will learn compassionate lawyer skills, mediation, creative problem solving, mentoring/coaching, leadership, legal philanthropy and maximum mind body and spirit self-care in addition to the most up-to-date information on the law.

Technology

The world is changing rapidly when it comes to technology. I used to work on a selectric typewriter with carbon paper. I dictated everything for someone to transcribe. I remember when desktop computers came out and my Dad got one for his law office. It was a huge albatross and he tried so hard to use it. I still see him behind it shouting "Sandy!" to his lifelong assistant sitting outside his office, asking her to come in and help him figure it out when he got stuck.

What I remember most was his determination to use technology. He would not allow himself to be left behind. Similarly, my office mate, attorney and mediator Dick Calkins who is over 80 years old and still comes to the office daily, worked tirelessly with my 27 year old daughter until he mastered his iPad.

More often than not, lawyers in the last phases of their practice are disinclined to try to master, or even dive in, to technology. As a result, the opportunity to use the creative brainpower for innovation in the law is a lost reservoir of wisdom.

Further, without the use of such things as Skype and Face Time, the ability to have those lawyers reach the populations of the underserved, such as poor or rural clients, is lost. The ability to effectively mentor the young law students is lessened because of disconnect on the basic language of technology. We must remember, however, like we teethed on teething toys, law students are coming up having been teethed with an iPhone softcover in their mouth.

Compassionate lawyers have a good solid working knowledge of technology. They are innovators. They work in all different media and dispense their wisdom through podcasts, webinars, and other innovative media. They use social media. They stay abreast of technological developments.

Technology is displacing some of the work traditionally reserved for lawyers. If we don't understand what the technology can do, how can we let our clients know the value added for having us involved in their problems?

We also have to be better organized and managed to be able to provide quality service with a quick turnaround. Lawyers are notorious for not returning calls in a timely fashion. People use telephones less than they used to. Compassionate lawyers use technology to streamline their calendars and provide quick turnaround for clients. If my clients need me I want them to be able to reach me, but still guard my boundaries for self-care. The only way to do this is by mastery of appropriate technology.

The future looks so much different than the current state of the legal profession. So lawyers, we have a choice. Will we embrace these changes with exhilaration and come together to become the problem solving, creative, compassionate lawyers the world has always expected us to be? Or will we stay stagnant and watch our profession become minimized?

Legacy

As part of my life's journey, people were continuously brought into my path to teach me. One was a spiritual mentor, Paul Leavenworth, who I met through my friend, Alicia. Paul is the author of several books and he offers workshops on many of them. I began to take Paul's courses in 2013.

I had gone through my second painful divorce and wanted to take special steps to heal my life. Paul's courses were instrumental in that healing (so was a course called, "WOW – Wholehearted Living" developed by Alicia). One of my favorite workshops was going through Paul's book *"The Extraordinary Power of a Focused Life, A Workbook for Leaders Who Want to Finish Well."* As part of the coursework I created a timeline of the events of my life, many of which I have described here. Simultaneously, I cross-referenced other life insights brought up through the guidance in the course.

On the last day of the workshop, I stared at the completed timeline containing the lists of my most devastating poor choices and life wounds, side-by-side with my triumphs, my gifts and blessings. My eyes filled with tears as I stared at it and listened to my heart.

"I wondered when you would see what you have just realized," my teacher Paul commented as he saw my emotional response.

"I was meant to be a lawyer," I told him as I saw the evidence laid out neatly in front of me. "Each part of my journey has led me to this place. I am a compassionate lawyer. And I have healed my life. Now I have to sound the call to other lawyers. We must reclaim our profession as a healing profession. As part of my legacy, I am to write a book and coach lawyers in how to practice law more compassionately."

Paul agreed. Shortly after that workshop I contracted with Paul to coach me to write this book. The writing journey has been intense, giving me new insights into myself, my life, and the legal profession. Self doubt has, at times, crept in. Healthy habits had to be more firmly rooted to sustain the fatigue of what seemed like an ominous writing project, with a possibly controversial message. Old messages of shame and inadequacy had to be replaced with the courage to speak my truth.

After reading *"The Compassionate Lawyer,"* my hope is that other lawyers will give themselves permission to operate as compassionate lawyers. Specifically, I hope this book will empower those who yearn to join the legal profession with a purpose of "helping people" to embrace the practice of law and help reclaim it for its original purpose.

Without having to make excuses for why they are "different."

Without feeling they are "less than" because they choose compassion instead of combat.

The goal of this book is twofold: to open up a dialogue about compassion in the law and to give lawyers a chance to reflect on compassion in their lives and their legal practices. Through shining a light on this subject, those of us who believe, as I do, that the law is a healing profession will consciously practice in a more compassionate way.

I see a world in which lawyers will first and foremost do as Abraham Lincoln suggested. We will discourage people from litigation, and instead empower clients to resolve conflict through peaceful methods led by compassionate lawyers.

My prayer is that I have had some small voice in reclaiming the word "lawyer" as one of respect and admiration and as one that depicts men and women who take their calling to the law seriously and recognize its sanctity.

More compassionate lawyer legacies

Dan Stamatelos

As always, I start with the legacy left by my father. Dan Stamatelos had a positive outlook and an exuberance for life, qualities he passed on to me and for which I am grateful.

As a child, Dad would take me to the nursing homes to visit with the elderly Greeks and those from the area of our hometown. I remember feeling proud of him because all the people we talked to loved him and were so grateful for our visits.

I have written about his interaction with clients and I will never forget at his funeral, when a man came up to my mother as she sat in the front pew of the church. The man kneeled, took my mother's hand and said "your husband saved my life." That memory has stuck in my head and I doubt his comment was because of some tremendous court verdict my Dad won. I would have to guess it was because my Dad dispensed compassion to that man in his time of need.

My Dad started a foundation at his church, providing all of the legal services to establish it for free, and he served as the church president. He served in numerous other civic capacities throughout his life and volunteered in countless ways. His efforts are vast and too numerous to mention.

The numbers of young people and law students Dad mentored were countless. He served as the president of the Board of Counselors at Drake Law School and was repeatedly recognized for his pro bono service in Polk County, Iowa.

Like all of us, Dad was not perfect. He suffered from a compulsive gambling addiction that he fought his entire adult life. He identified publicly as a recovering gambler, helping many people through the Gamblers Anonymous program. Undoubtedly others were inspired by a high profile individual who had the courage to step forward and admit he had struggles, just like we all do.

Most importantly he was a loving and present father to my two brothers and me, and a devoted husband to my mother until his death in 2001. He mentored me and helped me stay the course to my life as a compassionate lawyer. I always knew my father loved me.

Janet Reynoldson

The woman I saw at the Drake football game who encouraged me to go to law school also left a huge legacy. Jan had been an English teacher before deciding to go to law school. When she entered Drake University she was 42 years old and was still raising children. There were few women in her law school class in 1962.

Jan loved the practice of law, and her son Bob (also a lawyer) gave me a lot of information about her. He told me his mother would often discuss law over the kitchen table. She was the consummate trial lawyer, often having several bench trials and at least one jury trial, per month. The jury related to her because she was gracious and "talked their language."

Jan was a wonderful mentor to younger lawyers and is remembered for having "infinite patience" with them. More than one of the young lawyers she mentored became a judge. She was also a great listener and made you feel like you had her undivided attention "even on sundry things" reports Bob. She was also very self aware and had no airs about her, often making clients feel like they were members of the family.

Jan would never hesitate to cut her bill in order to make it work for the client. She expanded her practice into probate and estate planning after farm prices increased, so that she could help her rural clients structure their estates for the benefit of their family legacies.

Jan was on the Board of Trustees of the Drake Law School and was a leader at the Chamber of Commerce and her Methodist Church. Bob tells me that although Jan died in 1986, clients who come in to the law office still talk about her and express how much they miss her.

Judge Merrill Hartman

Judge Hartman was the judge who recruited me for pro bono work and mentored me when I was a baby lawyer in Dallas, Texas. From an excerpt of a 2006 blog by Eric Folkerth, via a Dallas Bar website article about Judge Hartman: "Often recognized for his many contributions to pro bono legal services, Hartman said he realized he had a gift as an attorney and knew that his services would likely be prohibitively expensive for the most vulnerable among our community to obtain. He also felt a strong moral responsibility as a Christian to love his fellow man. In 1983, Judge Hartman began to offer his legal assistance to the poor. He often told the story of two of his colleagues, and long-time friends, in an attempt to recruit other young lawyers to pro bono service.

When Judge Hartman decided to start a neighborhood legal clinic that would meet at the Dallas Bethlehem Center, he called his friend Will Pryor. The second volunteer to join them was Ellen Smith, at the time a plaintiff's lawyer with the firm then known as Carter Jones Magee Rudberg & Mayes. Judge Hartman, Will Pryor, Ellen Smith, and others would offer their services on Tuesday evenings, often helping mothers collect child support or obtain temporary restraining orders. They would then meet afterwards for Mexican food to recap the evening's events. It was not long thereafter that Ellen Smith suffered a terrible cycling accident. She was thrown from her bicycle and run over by a truck, breaking her back. Will Pryor and Judge Hartman visited her in the hospital daily; during this time Will and Ellen fell in love and were later married.

Judge Hartman went on to often recruit friends and colleagues from the Dallas Bar Association and Legal Services of North Texas to start additional clinics. He continued to enlist more volunteer lawyers to help represent low-income clients in court.

After becoming judge of the 303rd Family District Court in 1984, Hartman began holding court at legal clinics as a convenience to clients and their pro bono lawyers. He continued to hold court at clinics at least once a month to accommodate their needs by bringing access to justice for many who might not otherwise be able to make it to court.

Because of Judge Hartman's pioneering efforts, thousands of people in Dallas received free legal services. Hartman constantly recruited volunteer lawyers, taking time to visit law firms, Bar associations, and pro bono recruiting functions to speak about the importance of assisting low-income people in need of legal help."

Judge Hartman died in 2010.

Richard Calkins

Richard Calkins was the dean of the Drake University Law School when I attended there. We have shared a law office for ten years. I joke that he was responsive to being my office mate despite the fact he knew me as a lackluster law student. Dick has always been gracious with his time and wisdom, whenever I have needed an ear to listen. More importantly he has always encouraged me to follow my dreams in writing, and to practice law authentically.

He was the founder of the American Mock Trial Association, a national association that has set up competitions in mock trial in high schools and colleges across the country. He enlisted my Dad to serve on the board in AMTA's early years and they worked with others to expand the program often putting their own funds into the project when it was just beginning.

Dick was one of the first people trained as a mediator when I started my mediation company in the mid 1980's. He took his passion for mediation into the legal and education communities, establishing law school and college mediation competitions throughout the country. In 2014 one mediation tournament he held in Chicago drew participants from 20 countries. He has traveled extensively around the world to many destinations training mediators in those countries, often at his own cost.

Dick has mentored young people throughout his life. Many who are now high profile individuals in virtually all of the professions, participated in mock trial as a youth. He has also published numerous law review articles and several books.

Marsha Ternus

Marsha Ternus is the former Chief Justice of the Iowa Supreme Court, and the first woman appointed to that position. She encouraged me in the writing of this book and graciously read it through for early editing. Marsha also had me deliver a presentation on *The Compassionate Lawyer* to her restorative justice class at Grinnell College when I was beginning to write the book.

As Chief Justice, she had many notable accomplishments. During her tenure on the court Chief Justice Ternus made the improvement of court oversight of child welfare cases a priority for the Iowa Judicial Branch. She led an effort to form and then chaired the State Children's Justice Council. That council was a collaborative endeavor between the judicial branch, state agencies and private entities to institute reforms and improvements in the Iowa courts' processing of child welfare cases. She was the first recipient of an award for outstanding contributions to the welfare of children given by the Iowa Children's Justice Initiative.

While serving as Chief Justice, Marsha Ternus and her colleagues on the Iowa Supreme Court were so compassionate in their position for human rights they rendered the unanimous decision in Varnum v. Brien, 763 N.W.2d 862 (Iowa 2009), that held the state's limitation of marriage to opposite-sex couples violated the equal protection clause of the Iowa Constitution. She was the recipient of the 2012 John F. Kennedy Profile in Courage Award. Currently she is serving as the Director of The Harkin Institute for Public Policy and Citizen Engagement at Drake University.

The list of compassionate lawyer legacies goes on, and I invite stories of compassionate lawyers and legacy on our website. If you are one of these lawyers or know of one, please post their story at

www.thecompassionatelawyers.com
or
email me at
kim@attorneymediate.com.

Acknowledgements

To my three children **Danielle McCandless**, **Courtney McCandless** and **Clint McCandless**, for being generous with sharing their mother's time with the clients of Attorney Kim Stamatelos. I love you dearly and could not be more proud of the compassionate individuals you are.

To **Paul Leavenworth** for your patience, guidance and support as my coach and my friend. Without your obedience to God, this project would not have happened.

To **Father Andrew Barakos** for your prayers, encouragement, and spiritual support.

To compassionate lawyer **Laura Bramnick** for your friendship, unwavering support and the trips to the writing oasis in Flagstaff; and for being my kindred spirit.

To compassionate physician **Dr. Jean Lorentzen**, for getting me to wake up to the care of my physical self, and for your spiritual guidance.

To compassionate law student **Joslyn Sailer**, for your tireless brainstorming, editing and footnoting. I look forward to your work as a compassionate lawyer.

To all my former law students, lawyer friends and colleagues, with respect for the work you do to heal lives, and with gratitude that you have stayed in the profession despite its challenges.

To all my clients, past, present and future, with love and hope for continued healing.

Notes

Chapter 1 Introduction: My Journey To The Law

1. Stamatelos, Kimberly J. "Beyond Resolution Blog." http://attorneymedi ate.wordpress.com.

2. Stamatelos, Kimberly J. "Parenting Coordination: Moving Families Forward" *The Iowa Lawyer* 11 (Oct. 2012).

3. Schwartz Temple, Hollee. "Is the Integrative Law Movement the Next 'Huge Wave' for the Legal Profession?" ABA Journal: Law News Now (Aug. 1, 2013); available at http:// abajournal.com/magazine/article/ integrative_law_puts_passion_into_the_profession/.

Chapter 3 Have We Lost Our Way?

1. Flores, R., & Arce, R.M. "Why Are Lawyers Killing Themselves?" *CNN U.S.* (Jan. 20, 2014); *available at* http://www.cnn.com/2014/01/19/us/ lawyer-suicides/.

2. Ibid.

3. Ibid.

4. Ibid.

5. Cornette, M.M., & Busch, A.M. "Stress and Suicide" *The Charles E. Kubly Foundation: A Public Charity Devoted to Improving the Lives of Those Affected by Depression* (2014), *available at* http://charleskubly foundation.org/resource-center/resource-articles/stress-and-suicide/.

6. Flores, R., & Arce, R.M. "Why Are Lawyers Killing Themselves?" *CNN U.S.* (Jan. 20, 2014); *available at* http://www.cnn.com/2014/01/19/us/ lawyer-suicides/.

7. Cassens Weiss, D. "Lawyer Depression Comes Out of the Closet" *ABA Journal: Law News Now* (Dec. 13, 2007) *available at* http:www. abajournal.com/news/article/lawyer depression comes out of the closet.

8. Peterson, T.D., & Peterson, E.W. "Stemming the Tide of Law School Depression: What Law Schools Need to Learn from the Science of Positive Psychology." 9 *Yale Journal of Health Policy, Law, and Ethics* 357, 359 (2009).

9. Ibid.

10. Ibid.

11. Ibid.

12. Soonpaa, N.J. "Stress in Law Students: A Comprehesive Study of First-Year, Second-Year, and Third-Year Law Students." 36 *Conn. Law Review.* 353, 377-78 (2004).

13. Peterson, T.D., & Peterson, E.W. "Stemming the Tide of Law School Depression: What Law Schools Need to Learn from the Science of Positive Psychology." 9 *Yale Journal of Health Policy, Law, and Ethics* 2 (Mar. 3, 2013).

14. Ibid.

15. Ibid.

16. Lukasik, D. "In the Beginning: Depression in Law Schools." Lawyers with Depression (Sept. 3, 2013) *available at* http://www.lawyerswith depression.com/articles/in-the-beginning-depression-in-law-schools/.

17. Commission on Lawyer Assistance Programs. *American Bar Association, available at* http://www.americanbar.org/groups/lawyer assistance.html.

18. Childers, R.L. "Commission on Lawyer Assistance Programs: A Message From the Chair." *American Bar Association* (Jan. 27, 2010), *available at* http://apps.americanbar.org/legalservices/colap/colap-chair.html.

19. Angel, S.M. "The Burnout Pandemic: Accommodating Workaholism in the Practice of Law", Oklahoma Bar Association (2014), *available at* http://www.okbar.org/members/WorkLifeBalance/Articles/ BurnoutAngel.aspx.

20. Ibid.

21. Ibid.

22. Cassens Weiss, D. "Lawyers Second Most Likely Professional to Be in a Car Crash" *ABA Journal: Law News Now* (Dec. 7, 2009) *available at* http:www.abajournal.com/news/article/lawyers second most likely professional to be in a car crash

23. Ibid.

24. Ibid.

25. Krill, P. "Why Lawyers Are Prone to Suicide." *CNN Opinion* (Jan. 21, 2014), *available at* http://www.cnn.com/2014/01/20/opinion/krill lawyers-suicide/.

26. Peterson, T.D., & Peterson, E.W. "Stemming the Tide of Law School Depression: What Law Schools Need to Learn from the Science of Positive Psychology." 9 *Yale Journal of Health Policy, Law, and Ethics* 357, 358 (2009).

27. Ibid. 357, 359.

28. Ibid. 357, 368.

29. Albert, L. "Keeping Legal Minds Intact: Mitigating Compassion Fatigue Among Government Lawyers." 17 The Wisconsin Defender (2009), *available at* http://www.wisspd.ord/htm/ATPracGuides/WisDef/WinSpr09/MCF.pdf.

30. Ibid.

31. Ibid.

32. Ibid.

33. Molvig, D. "The Toll of Trauma." Wisconsin Lawyer (2011), *available at* http://www.wisbar.org/newspublications/wisconsinlawyer/pages/article.aspx?volume=84&issue=12&articleid=2356.

34. Ibid.

35. Flores, R., & Arce, R.M. "Why Are Lawyers Killing Themselves?" *CNN U.S.* (Jan. 20, 2014); *available at* http://www.cnn.com/2014/01/19/us/lawyer-suicides/.

36. Public Perceptions of Lawyers: Consumer Research Findings. *Section of Litigation. American Bar Association* 1 (2002), *available at* http://www.cliffordlaw.com/abaillinoisstatedelegate/publicperceptions1.pdf.

37. Ibid.

38. Ibid.

39. Ibid.

40. Ibid.

41. Ibid.

42. Ibid.

43. Ibid.

44. Ibid.

45. Ibid.

46. Ibid.

47. Ibid.

48. Ibid.

49. Ibid.

50. Presentation Survey – Lawyers/Legal System in America (2012), *available at* http://mcginnandcompany.com/Resources/Docs/Legal-Issues-Survey-120303.pdf.

51. Public Perceptions of Lawyers: Consumer Research Findings. *Section of Litigation. American Bar Association* 1 (2002), *available at* http://www.cliffordlaw.com/abaillinoisstatedelegate/publicperceptions1.pdf.

Chapter 4 **Moving Toward Compassion**

1. Luke 10:25-37

2. Splagchnizomai. *Bible Hub, available at* http://biblehub.comgreek/4697.htm.

3. *A Time To Kill*. Dir. Joel Schumacher. Perf. Matthew McConaughey and Sandra Bullock (1996).

4. Hawkins, D.R. *Power v. Force* (Hay House 2002) 67.

5. Ibid. 85-94.

6. Ibid. 76-83.

7. Ibid. 84.

8. Lemieux, C.P. Brené Brown Talks to the Shriver Report: The Power of Shame onWomen Living on the Brink. *The Shriver Report:Reporting From the Front Lines of Our Changing Lives* (Feb. 5, 2014), *available at* http://shriverreport.org/how-to-overcome-shame-when-on-the-brink-brene-brown/.

9. Wachtel, T. Defining Restorative. *International Institute for Restorative Practices: A Graduate School* 5 (2013), available at http://www.iirp.edu/pdf/Defining-Restorative.pdf.

10. Ibid.

11. Ibid.

12. Hawkins, D.R. *Power v. Force* (Hay House 2002) 84.

13. Levine, S. *Getting to Resolution: Turning Conflict into Collaboration* (Berrett-Koehler, 2009) 10.

14. Ibid. 9.

15. Brown, B. Brené Brown: The Safe Way to Share Your Shame Story. *HuffPost: Own Experts* (Nov. 20, 2013), *available at* http://www. huffingtonpost.com/2013/11/20/brene-brown-shame_n_4282679.html.

16. Coleman, D. Rich People Just Care Less. *New York Times, The Opinion Pages* (Oct. 5, 2013), *available at* http://opinionator.blogs.nytimescom/ 2013/10/5/rich-people-just-care-less/? php=true& type=blogs& r=0.

17. Ibid.

Chapter 5 **Mind, Body, Spirit**

1. Backes, D. Thomas Merton on Busyness and the Violence of Modern Life. *New Wood: Seeking the Infinite in a Finite World* (May 5, 2011), *available at* http://new-wood.blogspot.com/2011/05/thomas-merton-on-busyness-and-violence.html.

2. Cooper, B.B. 10 Simple Things You Can Do Today That Will Make You Happier, Backed by Science. *HuffPost: Science* (Nov. 11, 2013), *available at* http://www.huffingtonpost.com/belle-beth-cooper/10-simple-things-to-be-happy_b_4241824.html.

3. Ibid.

4. Goldsmith, B. Facebook Study Says Envy is Rampant On The Social Network. *HuffPost: Tech* (Jan. 22, 2013), *available at* http://www. huffingtonpost.com/2013/01/22/facebook-study-envy_n_2526549.html.

5. Dalai Lama XIV, Quotable Quote. GoodReads, available at https:// www.goodreads.com/quotes/525471-man-surprised-me-most-about-humanity-because-he-sacrifices-his-health.

6. The Clean Eating Team. What Is Clean Eating? *Clean Eating Magazine,* *available at* http://www.cleaneatingmag.com/food-healthy/food-and-health-news/what-is-clean-eating/.

7. Orloff, J. The Missing Piece to Overeating: Why Diets Fail. *Judith Orloff M.D.* (2005), *available at* http://www.drjudithorloff.com/Free-Articles/ Overeating.htm.

8. Peri, C. Coping With Excessive Sleepiness: 10 Things to Hate About Sleep Loss. WebMD, *available at* http://www.webmd.com/sleep-disorders/excessive-sleepiness-10/10-results-sleep-loss?page=3.

9. Johnston, S.L. Societal and Workplace Consequences of Insomnia, Sleepiness and Fatigue. *Medscape Multispecialty* (2005) *available at* http://www.medscape.org/viewarticle/513572.

10. O'Connor, A. How Sleep Loss Adds to Weight Gain. *New York Times* (Aug. 6, 2013), *available at* http://well.blogs.nytimes.com/2013/08/06/how-sleep-loss-adds-to-weight-gain/.

11. Ibid.

12. Ibid.

13. Physical Wellness. *Office of Alcohol and Drug Education* (2008), *available at* http://oade.nd.edu/wellness/physical-wellness/.

14. Winder, V. Exercise Makes You Think. *Taranaki Daily News Online* (Mar. 4, 2012), *available at* http://www.johnratey.com.files/2012Articles/Exercise-makes-you-think.pdf.

15. Ibid.

16. Ratry, J.J. & Hagerman, E. *Spark: The Revolutionary New Science of Excerisew and the Brain* (Little, Brown 2013) 85.

17. Ibid. 87.

18. Ibid. 245.

19. Oprah Explores How to Navigate Life Purpose with Caroline Myss. *Elevated Existence: Discovering the Devine in Body, Mind & Soul* (Jun. 29, 2012), *available at* http://www.elevatedexistense.com/blog/2012/05/29/oprah-explores-how-to-navigate-life-purpose-with-caroline-myss/.

20. Pneuma. *Bible Hub, available at* http://biblehub.com/greek/4151.htm.

21. Cooper, B.B. 10 Simple Things You Can Do Today That Will Make You Happier, Backed by Science. *HuffPost: Science* (Nov. 11, 2013), *available* at http://www.huffingtonpost.com/belle-beth-cooper/10-simple-things-to-be-happy_b_4241824.html.

22. Melcher, M.F. *The Creative Lawyer: A Practical Guide to Authentic Professional Satisfaction,* (American Bar Association 2007) 8.

23. Ibid. 9.

24. Chodron, P. *Taking the Leap: Freeing ourselves from Old Habits and Fears* (Shambhala Publications 2009) 2.

Chapter 6 **Caring**

1. Soren Kierkegaard, Quotable Quote. GoodReads, available at https://www.goodreads.com/quotes/24012-once-you-label-me-you-negate-me.

2. Philo of Alexandria, Quotable Quote. GoodReads, available at https://www.goodreads.com/quotes/31538-be-kind-for-everyone-you-meet-is-fighting-a-great.

3. Covey, S.R. *The 7 Habits of Highly Effective People* (Simon & Schuster 2004) 247-272.

4. Brown, B. *The Gifts of Imperfection: Let Go of Who You Think You're Supposed to Be and Embrace Who You Are* (Hazelden 2010) 10-12.

5. Brown, B. Shame v. Guilt. *Brené Brown* (Jan. 14, 2013), *available at* http://brenebrown.com/2013/01/142013114shame-v-guilt-html/.

6. Pink, D. *A Whole New Mind* (Riverhead Trade 2006) 46.

7. Ibid. 160.

8. Jones, S. Exploring the Dalai Lama's Teachings on Happiness. *Holton-Arms School* (Sep. 20, 2013), *available at* http://www.holtonarms.edu/page.cfm?p=1797&start=2&monthyear=09*2013&categoryID-0.

9. Charon, R. Narrative Medicine: A Model For Empathy, Reflection, Profession, and Trust. *JAMA* (2001), *available at* http://acmd615.pbworks.com/f/Narrative3.pdf.

10. Ibid.

11. Dr. Rita Charon: Biography. *Changing the Face of Medicine* (2013), *available at* http://www.nlm.nih.gov/changingthefaceofmedicine/phyisians/biography_58.html.

12. Ibid.

13. Gwosdezki, S. The Role Our Three Brains. *Integrated Wellness Therapies* (2014), *available at* http://integratedwellness.com.au/articles/three-brains/.

14. Hawkins, D.R. *Power v. Force,* (Hay House 2002) 84.

15. Ibid.

16. Brené Brown.

17. Brené Brown, Quotable Quote. GoodReads, available at https://www.goodreads.com/quotes/737201-courage-is-a-heart-word-the-root-of-the-word.

18. Ibid.

19. Ibid.

20. Brown, B. *The Gifts of Imperfection: Let Go of Who You Think You're Supposed to Be and Embrace Who You Are* (Hazelden 2010) 12.

21. Brown, B. Courage Is a Heart Word (and Family Affair). *PBS Parents: Expert Q&A, available at* http://www.pbs.org/parents/achive/2010/11/courage-is-a-heart-word-and-a.html.

Chapter 8 Empowering

1. Leavenworth, P.G. *Finishing Well: Life, Leadership and Legacy* (Convergence Publishing 2012) 1.

2. Collins, J. *How the Mighty Fall: And Why Some Companies Never Give In* (HarperCollins 2009) 20-21.

3. Stanley, P.D. & Clinton, J.R. *Connecting: The Mentoring Relationships You Need to Succeed* (NavPress 1992) 197-212.

4. Leavenworth, P.G. *Finishing Well: Life, Leadership and Legacy* (Convergence Publishing 2012) 7.

Chapter 9 Serving

1. YLD State Fair. *The Iowa tate Bar Association* (2012) *available at* http://isba.affiniscape.com/displaycommon.cfm?an=1&subarticle nbr=186.

2. Fisher, R., & Ury, W.L. *Getting to Yes: Negotiating Agreement Without Giving In* (Penguin Books 1991) 56-57.

3. Van Liew, F. *The Justice Diary: An Inquiry into Justice in the 21st Century available at* http://www.thejusticediary.com/author/admin/.

Chapter 11 Future

1. Johnson, J. Obama: Make Law School Two Years, Not Three. *USA Today* (Aug. 24, 2013), *available at* http://www.usatoday.com/story/news/nation/2013/08/24/newser-president-obama-law-school/2695265/.

2. Krieger, L.S. What We're Not Telling Law Students – And Lawyers – That They Really Need to Know: Some Thoughts-In-Action Toward Revitalizing the Profession from its Roots. 13 *J.L. Health* 1, 25 (1999).

3. Peterson, T.D., & Peterson, E.W. "Stemming the Tide of Law School Depression: What Law Schools Need to Learn from the Science of Positive Psychology." 9 *Yale Journal of Health Policy, Law, and Ethics* 357, 379 (2009).

4. Ibid.

5. Ibid.

6. Ibid.

7. Cassens Weiss, D. Lawyers In Prestige Positions Aren't as Happy as Those in Public Service Jobs, Study Finds. *ABA Journal: Law News Now* (Mar. 17, 2014), *available at* http://www.abajournal.com/news/article/lawyers_in_prestige_positions_arent_as_happy_as_those_in_public_service-job?utm_souce+maestro&utm_medium=email&utm_campaign=weekly_email..

8. Alvarez, L. Context and Culture. *Discovering Agreement: Bridging the Gap Between Vision and Action, Values and Systems, available at* http://www.discoveringagreement.com/for-lawyers/.

9. Ibid.

10. Pranis, K. *The Little Book of Circle Processes: A New/Pld Approach to Peacemaking* (Good Books 2005) 6.

11. Ibid.

12. Ricci, K. Courts Strategic Planning. *The American Institute of Architects* (Jul. 1, 2010) *available at* http://www.aia.org/akr/Resources/Documents/AIAB083531?ssSourceSiteId=null.

13. Ibid.

14. Ibid.

15. Staff, P. A Discussion with Frank Sander about Multi-Door Courthouse. *Harvard Law School: Program on Negotiation, Daily Blog* (Apr. 29, 2010), *available at* http://www.pon.harvard.edu/daily/a-discission-with-frank-sander-about-the-multi-door-courthouse/.

16. About the Authors: Frank E.A. Sander. *Wolters Kluwer: Law and Business, available at* http://www.aspenlawschool.com/books/goldbergsander/aboutThe Author.asp.

17. Sander, F.A. Dialogue Between Professors Frank Sander and Mariana Hernandez Crespo: Exploring the Evolution of the Multi-Door Courthouse. 5 *St. Thomas L. Rev. 665* (2008) *available at* http://ir.stthomas.edu/cgi/viewcontent.cgi?article=1164&context=ustlj.

18. Welcome to LMDC. *The Lagos Multi-Door Courthouse, available at* http://www.lagosmultidoor.org

Resources

Adams, Jeannie M. "Multi-Door Dispute Resolution Division." District of Columbia Courts; available at http://www.dccourts.gov/internet/superior/org_multidoor/main.jsf.

Angel, Steven M. "The Burnout Pandemic: Accommodating Workaholism in the Practice of Law", Oklahoma Bar Association (2014), available at http://www.okbar.org/members/WorkLifeBalance/Articles/BurnoutAngel.aspx.

Brown, Brené. The Gifts of Imperfection: Let Go of Who You Think You're Supposed to Be and Embrace Who You Are (2010).

Coleman, Daniel. "Rich People Just Care Less." New York Times, The Opinion Pages (Oct. 5, 2013); available at http://opinionator.blogs.nytimes.com/2013/10/05/rich-people-just-care-less/?_php=true&type=blogs&_r=0.

Collins, Jim. How the Mighty Fall: And Why Some Companies Never Give In (2009).

Cooper, Belle Beth. "10 Simple Things You Can Do Today That Will Make You Happier, Backed By Science," Huffington Post (Nov. 11, 2013); available at http://www.huffingtonpost.com/belle-beth-cooper/10-simple-things-to-be-happy_b_4241824.html.

Covey, Stephen R. 7 Habits of Highly Effective People (2005).

Fisher, Roger, and William L. Ury. Getting to Yes: Negotiating Agreement Without Giving In (1991).

Flores, Rosa, and Rose Marie Arce, "Why Are Lawyers Killing Themselves?" CNN U.S. (Jan. 20, 2014); available at http://www.cnn.com/2014/01/19/us/lawyer-suicides/.

Goldsmith, Belinda. "Facebook Study Says Envy is Rampant On The Social Network," Huffington Post (Jan. 22, 2013); available at http://www.huffingtonpost.com/2013/01/22/facebook-study-envy_n_2526549.html.

Grisham, John. A Time to Kill: A Novel (2009).

Hawkins, David. Power v. Force (2002).

Johnson, John. "Obama: Make Law School Two Years, Not Three." USA Today (Aug. 24, 2013).

Leavenworth, Paul G. The Discipleship and Mentoring Workbook: A Workbook for Younger Emerging Leaders (2011).

Levine, Stewart. Getting to Resolution: Turning Conflict into Collaboration (2009).

Melcher, Michael F. The Creative Lawyer (2007).

Myss, Caroline. Anatomy of the Spirit (1997).

O'Connor, Anahad. "How Sleep Loss Adds to Weight Gain." New York Times (Aug. 6, 2013); available at http://well.blogs.nytimes.com/2013/08/06/how-sleep-loss-adds-to-weight-gain/.

Orloff, Judith. "The Missing Piece to Overeating: Why Diets Fail." Judith Orloff, available at http://www.drjudithorloff.com/Free-Articles/Overeating.htm.

Peri, Camille. "Coping with Excessive Sleepiness: 10 Things to Hate About Sleep Loss." WebMD; available at http://www.webmd.com/sleep-disorders/excessive-sleepiness-10/10-results-sleep-loss.

Peterson, Todd David, and Elizabeth Walters Peterson, "Stemming the Tide of Law School Depression: What Law Schools Need to Learn from the Science of Positive Psychology." 9 Yale Journal of Health Policy, Law, and Ethics 2 (Mar. 3, 2013).

Pink, Daniel. A Whole New Mind (2006).

Ratey, John J. Spark: The Revolutionary New Science of Exercise and the Brain (2013).

Schwartz Temple, Hollee. "Is the Integrative Law Movement the Next 'Huge Wave' for the Legal Profession?" ABA Journal: Law News Now (Aug. 1, 2013); available at http://www.abajournal.com/magazine/article/integrative_law_puts_passion_into_the_profession/.

Stamatelos, Kimberly J. "Beyond Resolution Blog." http://attorneymediate.wordpress.com.

Stanley, Paul D., and J. Robert Clinton, Connecting: The Mentoring Relationships You Need to Succeed (1992).

Wachtel, Ted. "Defining Restorative, International Institute for Restorative Practices." (2013); available at http://www.iirp.edu/pdf/Defining-Restorative.pdf.

Weiss, Debra Cassens "Lawyer Depression Comes out of the Closet." ABA Journal: Law News Now (Dec. 13, 2007); available at http://www. abajournal.com/news/article/lawyer_depression_comes_out_of_ the_closet/.

"What is Clean Eating?" Clean Eating Magazine; available at http://www. cleaneatingmag.com/food-health/food-and-health-news/what-is-clean-eating/.

Zahorsky, Rachel M. "For Linda Alvarez, 'Attorney' Doesn't Have to Equal 'Adversary.'" ABA Journal: Legal Rebels (Sept. 26, 2012); available at http://www.abajournal.com/legalrebels/article/linda_alvarez_ agreeing_advocate.

Made in the USA
San Bernardino, CA
11 June 2014